Finding a Firm Foui

What

IN HEAVEN'S NAME

Is

Happening on Earth?

Finding a Firm Foundation in a Rapidly Changing World

William Calderwood, Ph.D.

Finding a Firm Foundation in a Rapidly Changing World

WHAT IN HEAVEN'S NAME IS HAPPENING ON EARTH? Finding a Firm Foundation in a Rapidly Changing World

Copyright © 2012 William Calderwood, Ph.D.

All rights reserved. No part of this publication may be reproduced, stored in a retrieval system, or transmitted in any form or by any means- electronic, mechanical, photocopy, recording, or any other – except for brief quotations in printed reviews, without prior permission from the publisher.

All Scripture references are taken from the Holy Bible, New International Version, Copyright 1973, 1978, 1984 by the International Bible Society, unless noted otherwise. Used by permission of Zondervan Publishing House.

Other Scripture quotations are from the following sources: Holy Bible: Contemporary English Version (CEV). New York: American Bible Society, 1995; J.B. Phillips Translation (JBP). The Macmillan Company, 1958, 1960, 1972; King James Version (KJV); The Living Bible (TLB). Wheaten, Ill.: Tyndale House Publishers,1971; New English Bible (NEB). Oxford University Press, Cambridge University Press, 1961, 1970; New Living Translation (NLT). Carol Stream, Ill.: Tyndale House Publishers, 2007; Today's English Version (TEV). American Bible Society, 1966, 1971, 1976; The Message. NavPress Publishing Group, Colorado Springs, Colorado, 2003.

ISBN -13:9781481155298

WFCI PRESS,
P. O. Box 907,
Coleman, Alberta,
Canada, TOK OMO.

Finding a Firm Foundation in a Rapidly Changing World

DEDICATION

To the memory of my Father and Mother, William and Wilhelmina Calderwood, who loved and served wholeheartedly the Lord Jesus.

Finding a Firm Foundation in a Rapidly Changing World

CONTENTS

Preface   1

PART ONE: WHAT IN HEAVEN'S NAME *HAS* HAPPENED ON EARTH?

1. GOD THE CREATOR *HAS* BEEN CREATING   7
2. GOD CHOSE A NATION   23
3. GOD MADE ETERNAL COVENANTS   39
4. A NEW COVENANT, A NEW HUMANITY, AND A NEW MEMORIAL   55

PART TWO: WHAT IN HEAVEN'S NAME *IS* HAPPENING ON EARTH?

5. THE LORD JESUS IS BUILDING HIS CHURCH!   69
6. THE RESURRECTION OF AN OLD ENEMY   85
7. ISRAEL'S SURVIVAL AND WORLDWIDE ISLAMIC EXPANSION   103
8. ISRAEL'S MIRACULOUS RESTORATION AND PRESERVATION   131

PART THREE: WHAT IN HEAVEN'S NAME *WILL* HAPPEN ON EARTH?

9. GOD WILL KEEP HIS COVENANT WITH ISRAEL   147
10. GOD WILL PROVIDE FOR OUR PROTECTION   171
11. CHRIST WILL COME AGAIN   187
12. A NEW HEAVEN AND A NEW EARTH   207

Finding a Firm Foundation in a Rapidly Changing World

PREFACE

The first decade of the twenty-first century has been an unsettling and tumultuous one throughout the world. Think of all the doom and gloom, worry and uncertainly that preceded the year 2000 – the Y2K phenomenon with all its end-of-the-world hysteria. Then came the world-impacting terrorist attack on the Twin Towers in New York City and on the Pentagon on September 11, 2001 – now just simply referred to as 9/11. After that headlines around the world were dominated by the war in Afghanistan, headlines that increasingly became anti-American as the Taliban's demise became possible and as other Islamic nations felt threatened and anxious about the awesome power of the U. S. military machine. These fears were heightened when the United States and Britain turned their attention to Saddam Hussein's dictatorship in Iraq, believing Saddam had the potential to supply world terrorists with nuclear weaponry.

There followed months and months of political wrangling and haggling within the United Nations Security Council as the U.S.- Britain Coalition tried to persuade the Security Council to use force, if necessary, to remove Saddam Hussein in order to weaken world terrorism and to strengthen world peace. We listened and watched as the U.N. nuclear weapons inspectors entered Iraq and as one frustration led to another, resulting in even more bickering and conflict within the Security Council – all of this broadcast around the world. Then came the split with the United Nations and the declaration of war with Iraq by the U.S.- Britain Coalition. France and Germany led the attack on the U.S. within the U.N. and my country, Canada, sided with France and Germany – breaking years of traditional solidarity and close friendship with the U.S. and Britain.

In spite of the success of the U.S.-Britain Coalition in ridding the world of an evil dictatorship and putting Iraq on the road to democracy, anti-Americanism is world-wide and seems to be increasing. Even in Canada, it's hard to find news media without a negative bias towards the United States. This anti-

What in Heaven's Name is Happening on Earth?

Americanism seems to be fueled in large part by the U.S. presence in Iraq, its traditional support of Israel and its commitment to protect Israel in the event of invasion by the millions of Arabs that surround her.

Add to the above, the ongoing war in Afghanistan, the economic collapse of 2008, all the political and military upheaval arising from the "Arab Spring" in Tunisia, Yemen, Egypt, Libya, Syria, and all the sickness and disease that spreads around the world as thousands of troops move from country to country, and more and more people travel and have easy access to places rarely visited in the past. Canada hasn't been immune to this: AIDS, the Norwalk virus, the West Nile virus, SARS, BSE (Mad Cow Disease) to name the more recent. On top of that, who would have predicted that our Prime Minister would initiate and promote a bill in parliament that would redefine marriage and endorse the homosexual lifestyle as something every bit a gift of God as heterosexuality? Some of us, as we've followed and watched the powerful homosexual lobby, knew the homosexual cause was gaining ground – but for it to happen so quickly! And for Canada to lead the way with only two other nations in the world redefining marriage! Who would have guessed it?

It's no wonder, then, that we're hearing the old clichés over and over again: "What on earth is happening in the world?" "In heaven's name, what's going on?" or "What's the world coming to?" Many of us are sensing that something is in the wind and that these are unusual times we're in. We will try to come to grips with this question about what's happening in our world by revising the old cliché, "What on earth is happening?" to "What in Heaven's Name is Happening on Earth?" You see, nothing has ever been or will be out of our God's loving control. We humans have been doing our best and our worst on this planet of ours but never for a minute has HIS-STORY been without the direction and purposes wrought in Heaven's Name. *"Who makes these things happen? Who controls human events?" asked the Lord, "I do! I am the Lord. I was there at the beginning; I will be there at the end"* (Isaiah 41:4 CEV).

The Lord's Prayer is being answered whether we realize it or not: His Kingdom has been and is coming and His will has been and is being done on earth! And His Kingdom will yet fully come and His will fully done on earth!

It's my prayer that as we study the Bible and discover (1) What *HAS* happened in Heaven's Name; (2) What *IS* happening in Heaven's Name; (3) What *WILL* happen in Heaven's Name, we will experience the peace and security, the joy and stability, the love and delightful expectation that our Father wants to lavish upon all His children.

This book evolved from a preaching series and Bible classes grappling with our Christian response to current events held over the past ten years at River of Life Community Church in Lethbridge. I am grateful for all the discussion, comments and constructive criticism engendered by the topic, which I have used throughout the text. The book has been designed to be used easily for weekly Bible studies. Special thanks are owed to Brett, Connie, Darrel, Diane, Jim, Ruth and Maidra for reading the first draft and providing useful comments and recommendations. I accept full responsibility, of course, for the ideas and conclusions expressed in this volume.

What in Heaven's Name is Happening on Earth?

Finding a Firm Foundation in a Rapidly Changing World

PART ONE

WHAT ON EARTH *HAS* HAPPENED IN HEAVEN'S NAME?

What in Heaven's Name is Happening on Earth?

Finding a Firm Foundation in a Rapidly Changing World

CHAPTER ONE

GOD THE CREATOR *HAS BEEN* CREATING!

As we come to the end of the account of creation, we stand in the place of wonder. Creation is past. And yet that does not mean that God ceases to be able to work into the world that he has made. God is not a prisoner of his own universe. By divine fiat God can change the universe that he has created just as by divine fiat he brought it into existence in the first place….And that God can work by fiat into the universe he has made is an important thing for twentieth-century men to comprehend.

Francis Schaeffer[1]

    The first revelation the Bible gives us of God is of God the Creator: "In the beginning God created the heavens and the earth" (Genesis 1:1). Genesis chapter one tells us that God created the universe by speaking it into existence: "And God

---

[1] *Genesis in Space and Time* (Downers Grove, Illinois 60515: InterVarsity Press, 1972), pp.56-57.

said, 'Let there be light,' and there was light" - six times it repeats the words "God said".

The word *God* is used 32 times in this first chapter in the Bible and is our English word for the Hebrew name *Elohim*.[2] It is one of the twelve names and compound names used in the Old Testament to further reveal to us puny humans the nature and character of God. How could we specks on a speck in the universe possibly grasp the nature of the God who spoke billions of stars and planets, millions upon millions of galaxies, into existence unless He revealed Himself to us in terms that we could comprehend – and even that, obviously, would only be a teeny-weeny glimpse of His greatness and glory. However, the wonderful Good News, the magnificent Gospel of Christ, is that we have a full revelation of the Father's heart in the Person of the Lord Jesus Christ. "Christ is exactly like God....God himself was pleased to live fully in his Son" (Colossians 1:15,19 CEV).

Elohim is used 2,570 times throughout the Bible and conveys the idea of the greatness and glory of God. It also contains the thought of creative and governing power, omnipotence and sovereignty.[3] This name reveals God as the Creator. The Apostle Paul preached to the people of Athens and gave this commentary on Genesis 1: "This God made the world and everything in it. He is Lord of heaven and earth...He doesn't need help from anyone. He gives life, breath, and everything else to all people. From one person God made all nations who live on earth, and he decided when and where every nation would be" (Acts 17:24-26 CEV).

---

[2] N. Stone, *The Names of God* (Chicago: Moody Press. 1944), p.12.

[3] Stone, p.12.

Finding a Firm Foundation in a Rapidly Changing World

What in Heaven's Name *has* happened in our world? God the Creator has been creating and proclaiming loudly His love and presence among us. "The heavens keep telling the wonders of God, and the skies declare what he has done. Each day informs the following day; each night announces to the next. They don't speak a word, and there is never a sound of a voice. Yet their message reaches all the earth, and it travels around the world"(Psalm 19:1-4 CEV).

The Bible also reveals that God created the earth for a specific purpose: for us humans! That's what it says in Genesis 1, after creating everything else and pronouncing it "good": "God said, 'Now we will make humans, and they will be like us. We will let them rule the fish, the birds, and all other living creatures.' So God created humans to be like himself; he made them men and women. God gave them his blessing and said: Have a lot of children! Fill the earth with people and bring it under your control…." (vs. 26-28 CEV)

There was nothing accidental or haphazard about our arrival on the scene. God planned and deliberately purposed to create us: "Long before he laid down earth's foundations, he had us in mind, had settled on us as the focus of his love, to be made whole and holy by his love" (Ephesians 1:4 *The Message*). Again, in Isaiah 45:18 "He who fashioned and made the earth…he did not create it to be empty but formed it to be inhabited…." And yet again: "Every desirable and beneficial gift comes out of heaven. The gifts are rivers of light cascading down from the Father of Light…He brought us to life using the true Word, showing us off as the crown of all his creatures" (James 1:17-18 *The Message*). So not only did He create us, but He purposely made us, focused His love upon us and made us the most important of all His creatures! Now that is something

What in Heaven's Name is Happening on Earth?

to get excited about! That is how the Lord of Heaven, the King of the Universe, sees you and me!

Not only were we deliberately planned by the Creator but each of us was designed to fulfill His plan for us – a plan unique and tailor-made for each of us. "For I know the plans I have for you," declares the Lord, "plans to prosper you and not to harm you, plans to give you hope and a future" (Jeremiah 29:11). Russell Kelfer's poem catches this truth so insightfully:

> You are who you are for a reason.
>
> You're part of an intricate plan.
>
> You're a precious and perfect unique design,
>
> Called God's special woman or man.
>
>
> You look like you look for a reason.
>
> Our God made no mistake.
>
> He knit you together within the womb,
>
> You're just what he wanted to make.
>
>
> The parents you had were the ones he chose,
>
> And no matter how you may feel,
>
> They were custom-designed with God's plan in mind,
>
> And they bear the Master's seal.

Finding a Firm Foundation in a Rapidly Changing World

> No, that trauma you faced was not easy.
>
> And God wept that it hurt you so;
>
> But it was allowed to shape your heart
>
> So that into his likeness you'd grow.
>
> You are who you are for a reason,
>
> You've been formed by the Master's rod.
>
> You are who you are, beloved,
>
> Because there is a God![4]

God created you for a purpose! That we know that is of the highest importance, if we want peace and joy in our lives, lives meaningful, purposeful and fruitful. In *The Purpose Driven Life*, Rick Warren writes about the importance of knowing God's purpose for our lives. He states and discusses:

> Knowing your purpose gives meaning to your life
>
> Knowing your purpose simplifies your life.
>
> Knowing your purpose focuses your life.

---

[4] Rick Warren, *The Purpose Driven Life*,(Grand Rapids, Michigan: Zondervan, 2002), pp.25-26.

What in Heaven's Name is Happening on Earth?

Knowing your purpose motivates your life.

Knowing your purpose prepares you for eternity.[5]

Paul exhorted the Philippian Christians in a similar fashion: "I've got my eye on the goal, where God is beckoning us onward – to Jesus. I'm off and running, and I'm not turning back. So let's keep focused on that goal, those of us who want everything God has for us. If any of you have something else in mind, something less than total commitment, God will clear your blurred vision – you'll see it yet! Now that we're on the right track, let's stay on it" (Philippians 3:13-16 *The Message*).

What in Heaven's Name *has been* going on in the world? Our loving Lord, full of mercy and grace, has been searching for and finding millions of His children who have eagerly grasped the plan and purpose He offers them. Are you one of the millions who have readily entered into the Lord's purpose and plan for your life? If you have, know that it brings great pleasure to the Lord. I'm sure the writer of 3 John 4 reflected the heart of God when he wrote "I have no greater joy than to hear that my children are walking in the truth."

To speak further about bringing pleasure to the Lord, do you know that He created us for His pleasure? We are told in Revelation 4:11 that heavenly worshippers will praise Him: "You created everything, and it is for your pleasure that they exist and were created" (*New Living Translation*). Again, even more directly, in Psalm 149:4 that "the Lord takes pleasure in his people" and in Ephesians 1:4 "Because of his love God had already decided that through Jesus Christ he would make us his

---

[5] *Ibid.,* pp. 30-34.

children – this was his pleasure and purpose"(*Today's English Version*).

That being the case – that He created us for His pleasure – wouldn't it be smart to find out what we can do to please Him? The Apostle Paul certainly thought so: "Figure out what will please Christ, and then do it," he wrote (Ephesians 5:10 *The Message*). So let's do that. Let's see what the Bible says we must do to please the Lord:

Be like Noah!

Genesis 6:8 "Noah was a pleasure to the Lord." (*Living Bible*).

Honour Him and trust His love!

Psalm 147:11 "He takes pleasure in those that honor Him; in those who trust in His constant love" (TEV).

Have faith!

Hebrews 11:6 "Without faith it is impossible to please God".

Be doers and not only believers!

James 2:24 "You can now see that we please God by what we do and not only by what we believe" (CEV)

What in Heaven's Name is Happening on Earth?

Praise and glorify God in song and with thanksgiving!

    Psalm 69:30-31 "I will praise God's name in song and glorify him with thanksgiving. This will please the Lord."

Be godly (or Christlike)!

    Psalm 37:23 "The steps of the godly are directed by the Lord. He delights in every detail of their lives" (NLT).

Above all else, earnestly desire to please the Lord Jesus!

    2 Corinthians 5:9 "More than anything else, however, we want to please him, whether in our home here or there" (TEV).

Be wise – long to please the Lord Jesus!

    Psalm 14:2 "The Lord looks down from heaven on all mankind to see if there are any who are wise, who want to please God" (LB).

    "Bringing enjoyment to God, living for his pleasure, is the first purpose of your life," declares Rick Warren. "When you fully understand this truth, you will never again have a problem with feeling insignificant. It proves your worth. If you are *that* important to God, and he considers you valuable enough to keep with him for eternity, what greater significance could you have? You are a child of God, and you bring pleasure to God like nothing else he has ever created."[6]

HE CREATED THE NATIONS

We must also understand and acknowledge that the nations are never out of His control. Although it is the nations that provoke wars by aggression, greed and selfishness, that are at the bottom of the turmoil and conflict in the world, that persecute and kill God's people, the Bible tells us that "from one man he made every nation of men, that they should inhabit the whole earth; and he determined the times set for them and the exact places where they should live" (Acts 17:26).

The Lord promised Abraham that his descendants would become a great nation and would bless all the nations (Genesis 12:1-2). That nation, of course, was Israel. He also promised Hagar, Abraham's concubine, that her son Ishmael would be the father of a great nation (21:13,18). Our God could make promises like that because He created all the nations! Genesis 11 relates the story of how the Lord thwarted the rebellion against Him at the Tower of Babel and scattered His children all over the earth into people groups with distinctive languages. "To the Lord," observed the prophet Isaiah, "all nations are merely a drop in the bucket or dust on balance scales" (Isaiah 40:15 CEV). Likewise the Psalmist exclaimed in praise, "The Lord is far above all the nations"! (113:4 CEV)

---

[6] Warren, p. 63.

What in Heaven's Name is Happening on Earth?

Not only did He create the nations, but our God controls them! "People all over the world will turn and worship you because YOU ARE IN CONTROL, THE RULER OF ALL NATIONS," exulted King David in Psalm 22:27-28 (CEV). How does He control the nations? The Bible reveals that

- He watches over the nations: "His mighty power rules forever, and nothing the nations do can be hidden from him. So don't turn against God" (Psalm 66:7 CEV).
- He guides the nations: "May the nations be glad and sing for joy, for you rule the peoples justly and guide the nations of the earth" (Psalm 67:4 CEV).
- He raises up and brings down the nations: "He sifts the nations and destroys them"(Isaiah 30:28 CEV); "I will send nations to attack you [Tyre], like waves crashing against the shore" (Ezekiel 26:3 CEV); "I will cast out the nations before you" (Exodus 34:24).
- He brings nations together: "He will settle arguments between nations" and they will make peace with each other (Isaiah 2:4 CEV).
- He "shakes" and "gathers" the nations: Haggai 2:7, Joel 3:2.
- All the nations one day will bow in submission to Him: "You created each nation, and they will bow down to worship and honor you" (Psalm 86:9 CEV); "I...will gather all nations and tongues, and they will come and see my glory" (Isaiah 66:18-19); "Our Lord, great and powerful, you alone are God. You are the King of the nations" (Jeremiah 10:6-7 CEV).

Finding a Firm Foundation in a Rapidly Changing World

Our God created the earth and all its peoples and has never ever relinquished ownership of it. "The earth is the Lord's, and everything in it, the world, and all who live in it," states Psalm 24:1. Neither has he ever ceased working out His plan and purpose in His Creation, in His children, and in the nations. But there is one nation that is closer to His heart than any other – the nation of Israel. Our next chapter is about why and how that came to be.

SUGGESTED ORDER FOR SMALL GROUPS

APPROACHING WITH PRAISE AND WORSHIP

Choruses or prayers of praise, thanksgiving and adoration

PRAYER TIME

Prayers of confessions, petition & intercession

BIBLE WARM-UP: The Old Testament Names of God

Elohim (pronounced el-lo-heem): God the Mighty One, Creator, great and glorious. Translated in the Bible as "God".

MEMORY VERSE

"*In the beginning God created the heavens and the earth.*" Genesis 1:1

What in Heaven's Name is Happening on Earth?

DAILY BIBLE READINGS: WORDS & THOUGHTS FOR FURTHER REFLECTION

Day 1: Isaiah 1:1-17

_____

_____

Day 2: Isaiah 1:18-31

_____

_____

Day 3: Isaiah 2

_____

_____

Day 4: Isaiah 3

_____

_____

Day 5: Isaiah 4

_____

_____

Finding a Firm Foundation in a Rapidly Changing World

Day 6: Isaiah 5:1-17

_____

_____

Day 7: Isaiah 5:18-30

DISCUSSION QUESTIONS

1. Read Genesis 1. What is the first thing the Bible tells us about God?

2. How did God create the world?

3. Compare John 1:3 with Genesis 1. What further information about creation does this passage give us?

4. Discuss the meaning of the Hebrew word, *Elohim*.

5. Read Ephesians 1:4-5. What had God in mind before the creation?

6. Since we are created for God's pleasure, name some of the ways we can please Him. Discuss.

7. What is God's relationship to the nations of the world? Check out some of the Scriptures in the Textbook

.

Finding a Firm Foundation in a Rapidly Changing World

CLOSING PRAYER: Our Father, thank you for creating us to be like you. We come confessing the many times we've disappointed you and grieved your heart by living far below your loving example. Please forgive us, our gracious Father, and help us more and more to live lives that please you. That's the commitment we make right now, that we are going to find out what pleases you and we're going to do it. Please help us. In the Mighty Name of the Lord Jesus, we pray. Amen.

What in Heaven's Name is Happening on Earth?

Finding a Firm Foundation in a Rapidly Changing World

CHAPTER TWO

GOD CHOSE A NATION

The story of Jewish identity across the millennia against impossible odds is a unique miracle of cultural survival. Where are the Sumerians, the Babylonians, the Assyrians today?...However miraculous Jewish survival may be, the greater miracle is surely that the Jews developed a whole new way of experiencing reality, the only alternative to all ancient worldviews and all ancient religions. If one is ever to find the finger of God in human affairs, one must find it here.

Thomas Cahill [7]

    Nothing takes God by surprise! When Eve was deceived by the serpent in the Garden of Eden and she and Adam

---

[7] The Gifts of the Jews (New York: Nan A. Talese Doubleday, 1998), p. 246.

rebelled against the Lord, He had a plan already formed to reverse the curse of suffering, pain, death and alienation and to restore His children to living in loving relationship with Him once again. Paul told the Ephesian Christians that they had been chosen in the Lord Jesus "before the creation of the world to be holy and blameless" in God's sight (1:4 NIV). The Apostle Peter reminds us that we were rescued by "the precious blood of Christ, a lamb without blemish or defect...chosen before the creation of the world" (1 Peter 1:19-20. See also Revelation 13:8).

No sooner had Adam and Eve disobeyed Him, when the Lord came to visit them (Genesis 3). His call "Where are you?" wasn't for His benefit – He knew exactly where they were – it was for their benefit: they needed to know what they had done and where they were in their relationship with their loving Lord. After hearing their excuses, Adam blaming Eve and Eve blaming the serpent, the Lord cursed the serpent and explained the curse Adam and Eve had brought upon themselves. But at the conclusion of cursing the serpent, the Lord uncovered the plan that was already in the making. He informed Satan that one of Eve's descendants "will strike you on the head, and you will strike him on the heel" (vs. 15). This is the first prophecy about the coming Saviour, the Lord Jesus, who would strike the devil a fatal blow to the head, while the devil would only "bruise his heel"(Revised Standard Version). It is not exaggerating to say that the rest of the Bible was written to reveal how that prophecy was fulfilled and is being fulfilled.

GOD CHOSE A MAN

In the process of making and choosing a nation for His plan and purpose, God chose a man, Abraham. Genesis 11 opens with the Tower of Babel and consequent forming of nations around the world and closes with the arrival of Terah, the father of Abraham, in the city of Haran. Terah had left his home city, Ur in Chaldea (present day Southern Iraq), heading for the land of Canaan, but decided to settle at Haran, about halfway to Canaan (11:26-32). He brought with him his son, Abraham; his daughter-in-law, Sarai, Abraham's wife; and his grandson, Lot.

With no more information than that given about Abraham, we are suddenly and abruptly informed that "The Lord said to Abraham: Leave your country, your family, and your relatives and go to the land that I will show you. I will bless you and make your descendants into a great nation. You will become famous and be a blessing to others. I will bless anyone who blesses you, but I will put a curse on anyone who puts a curse on you. Everyone on earth will be blessed because of you" (Genesis 12:1-3 CEV). The martyr Stephen in Acts 7:2-5 stated that the Lord had spoken to Abraham in Chaldea and before he settled in Haran with his father.

Why Abraham? There are at least three reasons why Abraham was chosen to be the father of the nation of Israel:

One, the sovereignty of God. For His own reasons, the Lord simply picked Abraham as the person for this specific plan and purpose, as He did Noah before Abraham and Moses and a host of others after him. "Who can measure the wealth and wisdom and knowledge of God?" the Apostle Paul asks in awe, "Who can understand his decisions or explain what he does? Has anyone known the thoughts of the Lord or given him advice?" (Romans 11:33-34 CEV)

Two, Abraham was obviously available. God spoke and Abraham heard and listened. Genesis chapters 12 -25 portray clearly Abraham as a man who listened to and obeyed the Lord. So much so that James 2:23 tells us that "he was called the friend of God". Friends love to be available for each other! I wonder how many times I have missed opportunities to serve the Lord because I just wasn't available and was caught up with something ultimately trivial in light of eternity? We have to hear before we can obey: are we listening?

Three, Abraham exercised his faith. God told him to leave his country, family and relatives and go to a land later to be revealed. And Abraham left not knowing where he was going (Genesis 12:4-5). Hebrews 11:8 tells us that was faith: Abraham believed or had faith that the Lord could be trusted and would tell him as he went. Later on, in Genesis 15:1-6, the Lord again promises to protect and greatly reward Abraham and to make his descendants as numerous as the stars in the sky – and Abraham's simple faith accepted that the Lord would be true to His word. "Abram believed the Lord," says the Bible, "and the Lord was pleased with him" (vs.6 CEV). No wonder he is called the Father of the Faithful and used by Paul and James as the biblical model *par excellence* of someone exercising faith (Romans 4:1-25; James 2:21-23).

Abraham – along with Moses (Exodus 33:11) – was called the friend of God and a myriad of others, from Enoch to David ("a man after God's own heart", Acts 13:22) to the Lord Jesus' inner circle to a blood-washed throng of Christian martyrs and servants right up to the present, have lived vibrantly in intimate relationship with the Lord.

What in Heaven's Name *has been* happening on earth? Our God has been choosing friends and millions have been reveling in His friendship! Am I? Are you?

GOD CHOSE ISRAEL

God's plan of salvation for His children to break the curse of Adam and Eve's rebellion and disobedience and to restore the loving and intimate relationship that began in the Garden of Eden centred on the coming of the Lord Jesus to earth, the Incarnation of God the Son. Hebrews 10:5-7 provides the following insight: "When Christ came into the world, he said to God, 'Sacrifices and offerings are not what you want, but you have given me my body. No, you are not pleased with animal sacrifices and offerings for sin.' Then Christ said, 'And so, my God, I have come to do what you want, as the Scriptures say.'" God the Son came amongst us and shared our physical nature, confining Himself in a human body for thirty-three years with which, it seems, He will be forever identified (see John 20:24-28; 21:11-14).

In order to be fully human, the Lord Jesus had to be born into a human family at a particular time and at a specific location. He had to be born within some nation or people group. God chose Israel and, therefore, Jesus was born a Jew. If the God had chosen the ancient and great worldly kingdom of Egypt, then the Lord Jesus would have been an Egyptian. Or if He had chosen Italy, He would have been Italian; if France, then

French; in Scotland, then Scottish. But He didn't choose Egypt, Italy, France or Scotland: God chose Israel.

Why Israel? I find at least four reasons:

One, God chooses whom He chooses and feels no obligation to consult anyone or to explain His reasons: He is the Sovereign Lord. Isaiah puts that truth in these words: "Has anyone told the Lord what he must do or given him advice? Did the Lord ask anyone to teach him wisdom and justice? Who gave him knowledge and understanding?....The holy God asks, 'Who compares with me? Is anyone my equal?'" (Isaiah 40:13-14, 25 CEV)

Two, God chose Israel because of His promise to Abraham. "Israel, you are my servant," prophesied Isaiah, "I chose you, the family of my friend Abraham...I brought you here and said, 'You are my chosen servant, I haven't forgotten you" (Isaiah 41:8-9 CEV). Psalm 105:40-42 reminds us that when Israel cried out to the Lord for food and water in the wilderness, "he sent more birds than they could eat. God even split open a rock, and streams of water gushed into the desert. GOD NEVER FORGOT HIS SACRED PROMISE TO HIS SERVANT ABRAHAM"(CEV; emphasis added; also Deuteronomy 7:7;9:6).

Three, God chose Israel because it had the least potential of all the nations. Moses confronted Israel with that stark reality: "Israel, you are the chosen people of the Lord your God. There are many nations on this earth, but he chose only Israel to be his very own. YOU WERE THE WEAKEST OF ALL NATIONS, but the Lord chose you because he loves you and because he had made a promise to your ancestors. Then with his mighty arm, he rescued you from the king of Egypt, who had made you his slaves" (Deuteronomy 7:6-8 CEV, emphasis added). Later on, Moses felt it necessary to remind Israel that after the Lord helps them conquer Canaan and inhabit the Promised Land, "don't think he did it because you are such good people. You aren't good – you are stubborn! No, the Lord is going to help you, because the nations that live there are evil, and because he wants to keep the promise he made to your ancestors Abraham, Isaac, and Jacob" (Deut. 9:4-6 CEV).

Four, God chose Israel simply because He loved her. Moses stated it clearly and emphatically to Israel: "the Lord chose you because he loves you" (Deut. 7:7). Isaiah said the same thing but more elaborately and more beautifully: "I, the Lord, created you and formed your nation. Israel, don't be afraid. I have rescued you. I have called you by name; now you belong to me. When you cross deep rivers, I will be with you, and you won't drown. When you walk through the fire, you won't be burned or scorched by the flames….To me, you are very dear, and I love you. That's why I gave up nations and people to rescue you" (43:1-2, 4 CEV)

.

THE LAND AND THE CITY

Every nation is identified by its land and has a capital city. Israel is located along the coast at the eastern end of the Mediterranean Sea. God gave the land to Israel after promising it to Abraham and his descendants: "I will give your descendants the land east of the Shihor River on the border of Egypt as far as the Euphrates River" and, again, "I will always keep the promise I have made to you and your descendants, because I am your God and their God. I will give you and them the land in which you are now a foreigner. I will give the whole land of Canaan to your family forever, and I will be their God"(Genesis 15:18-19;17:7-8 CEV).

When the mantle of leadership was passed on from Moses to Joshua, and just before Israel entered the Promised Land, the Lord said to Joshua, "I will give you every place where you set your foot, as I promised Moses. Your territory will extend from the desert and from Lebanon to the great river, the Euphrates – all the Hittite country – and to the Great Sea [the Mediterranean] on the west….Be strong and courageous, because you will lead these people to inherit the land I swore to their forefathers to give them" (Joshua 1:3-6).

It was around the 13th century B.C. when Joshua led the army of Israel into Canaan and defeated the Canaanite peoples: the Kenites, the Kenizzites, the Kadmonites, the Hittites, the Perizzites, the Rephaites, the Amorites, the Canaanites, the Girgashites, and the Jebusites (Genesis 15:19 CEV). Israel settled in the land of Canaan and consolidated the kingdom under the "Judges." Then under the Monarchy, especially under the first two kings, Saul and David, the unification of the country was accelerated and completed. After David came his son, Solomon, whose reign saw the building of the Temple in Jerusalem, the rapid expansion of international trade, and forty years of peace. Solomon's reign has been looked upon as the high point of Israel's national glory. [8]

It was King David who captured the Jebusite city of Jerusalem and made it Israel's capital. He did that at the express order from the Lord. It was God who chose Jerusalem and not just for the governing of Israel but for His own special

---

[8] Carta's *Historical Atlas of Israel*.

possession and purposes. King Solomon praised the God of Israel because He "kept his promise to make my father David the king of Israel. The Lord also promised him that Jerusalem would be the city where his temple will be built, and now that promise has come true" (2 Chronicles 6:6 CEV). Furthermore, the Lord speaks about Jerusalem as "the city where I have chosen to be worshipped" and the city "I chose to be mine" (2 Kings 23:27; 1 Kings 11:36 CEV). In Zechariah 3:2 the Lord said, "Jerusalem is my chosen city."

The Lord chose Israel, gave her land and a great city, to be the means through which the Messiah, the Lord Jesus, would come into the world and because of that she had and has a special place in His heart. "You are my servant," the Lord assures Israel, "I chose you…You are my chosen servant. I haven't forgotten you. Don't be afraid. I am with you. Don't tremble with fear. I am your God. I will make you strong, as I protect you with my arm and give you victories….I am the Lord your God, I am holding your hand, so don't be afraid. I am here to help you" (Isaiah 41:8-10, 13 CEV).

GOD'S PROGRESSIVE REVELATION OF HIMSELF

From Genesis to Revelation, the Bible is an ongoing revelation of the personal attributes of God, of how He desires a loving relationship with His children, and how they can enter and enjoy that loving relationship. One of the ways the Lord does that is through the different names and compound names He uses in the Old Testament to reveal diverse aspects of His character and of His dealings with us.

What in Heaven's Name is Happening on Earth?

We noticed the use of the name *Elohim* (pronounced el-lo-heem) earlier on, meaning God the Mighty One, Creator, great and glorious. The others are as follows:

Jehovah or Yahweh (pronounced je-ho-vah; ya-wey) : the God who was, is and always will be; the God who always exists, eternal and unchangeable.

El-Shaddai (el-shad-di): God Almighty or Almighy God, God the Omnipotent One.

Adonai (pronounced a-do-ni): the God who is Master, Lord, Owner of all that exists.

Jehovah-jireh (je-ho-vah yeer-eh): God our Provider.

Jehovah-rophe (je-ho-vah ro-phay): God our Healer.

Jehovah-nissi (je-ho-vah nis-see): God our Banner or Ensign or Standard.

Jehovah-M'Kaddesh (je-ho-vah m-kad-desh):God our Sanctifier.

Jehovah-shalom (je-ho-vah shal-lom): God our Peace.

Jehovah-tsidkenu (je-ho-vah tsid-kay-noo): God our Righteousness.

Jehovah-rohi (je-ho-vah ro-ee): God our Shepherd.

Jehovah-shammah (je-ho-vah sham-mah): God the Ever-Present one, the God who is there.

What in Heaven's Name *has been* happening on earth? God has been revealing Himself to us from the very beginning through Creation and a multitude of other ways. He has manifested Himself to us effectively in these Old Testament names. "There is a wonderful and significant order to these compound names of Jehovah as they appear in the Scriptures…." observed Nathan Stone in *NAMES OF GOD*, "In these names there is a progressive revelation of Jehovah meeting every need as it arises in the experiences of His redeemed people – saving, sustaining, strengthening, sanctifying, and so on; and not only for the redeemed of that day but for God's saints in all ages" (p.70).

SUGGESTED ORDER FOR SMALL GROUPS

APPROACHING WITH PRAISE AND WORSHIP

Choruses or prayers of praise, thanksgiving & adoration.

PRAYER TIME

Prayers of confession, petition & intercession

BIBLE WARM-UP: The Old Testament Names of God

Jehovah or Yahweh (pronounced je-ho-vah; ya-wey): the God who was, is and always will be; the God who always exists, eternal and unchangeable. Trans. In the Bible as "LORD".

What in Heaven's Name is Happening on Earth?

MEMORY VERSE

Genesis 12:3 *"I will bless those who bless you, and whoever curses you I will curse; and all people on earth will be blessed through you."*

DAILY BIBLE READINGS: WORDS & THOUGHTS FOR FURTHER REFLECTION

Day 1: Isaiah 6

_____
_____

Day 2: Isaiah 7

_____
_____

Day 3: Isaiah 8

_____
_____

Day 4: Isaiah 9

Finding a Firm Foundation in a Rapidly Changing World

Day 5: Isaiah 10:1-19

Day 6: Isaiah 10:20-34

Day 7: Isaiah 11

DISCUSSION QUESTIONS

1. How did God handle Adam's and Eve's disobedience in Genesis 3? Discuss the "the blaming each other" part of it.

2. Read Genesis 12 and compare with Romans 4. How did Abraham respond and what was the outcome of his response?

3. Give the three reasons mentioned why Abraham was chosen to be the father of Israel?

4. According to Deuteronomy 7:7-9, why did God choose Israel?

5. Read Isaiah 41:8-10. What promise does God give to Israel? What are some of the things He has done and will do for Israel?

6. Discuss the four reasons why God chose Israel.

7. God revealed Himself progressively in the Old Testament in 12 names and compound names. Which names are particularly meaningful for you?

CLOSING PRAYER: Lord Jesus, Glorious Son of our Father, thank you for revealing yourself to us, for finding us and bringing us home. You've chosen us in spite of our weaknesses and failures and called us to serve you. Thank you for the wonderful names through which you have shown us the many facets of your loving and gracious heart. Help us to follow hard after you, Lord Jesus, and ever and always deepen and strengthen our friendship and communion with you. In your Holy and Lovely Name, Amen.

What in Heaven's Name is Happening on Earth?

Finding a Firm Foundation in a Rapidly Changing World

CHAPTER THREE

GOD MADE ETERNAL COVENANTS

The notion of a covenant is unfamiliar today. But the concept of covenant is utterly basic to our understanding of Scripture. In OT times this complex concept was the foundation of social order and social relations, and it was particularly the foundation for an understanding of humanity's relationship with God.

Lawrence O. Richards[9]

Webster's Dictionary defines a covenant as: 1. Usually a formal, solemn, and binding agreement; 2. a written agreement or promise usually under seal between two parties especially for the performance of some action. When it comes to covenants between God and us, one theologian states that such a covenant is "an unchangeable, divinely imposed legal

---

[9] *New International ENCYCLOPEDIA OF BIBLE WORDS* (Grand Rapids, Michigan: Zondervan Publishing House, 1991), p. 193.

agreement between God and man that stipulates the conditions of their relationship." He explains that "divinely imposed" means that we can "never negotiate with God or change the terms of the covenant." We can only accept the covenant obligations or reject them. He goes on to point out that the Old and New Testament translators did not use the ordinary Greek word for contracts or agreements in which both parties were equal, but instead a less common word that emphasized that the terms of the covenant were laid down by one of the parties only.[10]

WITH ADAM AND NOAH

Our God is a covenant-making God! The first covenant the Lord made in the Bible is in Genesis 2:15-17, sometimes called "The Covenant of Works," when Adam was commanded not to eat from the tree of the knowledge of good and evil. Although the word "covenant" is not used here, it is used in Hosea 6:6-7 when the prophet reminds Israel that "Like Adam, they have broken the covenant." Then in Genesis 8:21-22; 9:1-17, after the Flood. Noah and his family were no sooner off the Ark, it seems, when Noah built an altar and offered sacrifices to the Lord. This pleased the Lord so much that He declared: "Never again will I punish the earth for the sinful things its people do. All of them have evil thoughts from the time they are young, but I will never destroy everything that breathes, as I did this time. As long as the earth remains, there will be planting and harvest, cold and heat; winter and summer,

---

[10] Wayne Grudem, *Systematic Theology*, (Leicester, England: Inter-Varsity Press, 1994), p. 515.

day and night." The Lord went on to address Noah and his sons specifically, covenanting with them in these words: "I am going to make a solemn promise to you and to everyone who will live after you….I promise every living creature that the earth and those living on it will never again be destroyed by a flood. The rainbow that I have put in the sky will be my sign to you…that I will keep this promise forever" (CEV). When God communicates, He communicates! There is no one who has not seen and marveled at the rainbow. Notice also: there were no conditions attached to this. God simply declared this is what HE was going to do. Period.

WITH ABRAHAM

God was true to His word with Abraham and did guide and direct him to the Promised Land. He asked Abraham to obey Him first by leaving his family and country and would then show him his destination. It was the beginning of an intimate relationship between the Lord and Abraham and within a short time God had made a covenant with him. "On that day the Lord made a covenant with Abram," we read in Genesis 15:18, "and said, 'To your descendants I give this land, from the river of Egypt to the great river, the Euphrates." This was repeated later on, as if the Lord was making sure there would be no mistake about it: "God said to him, "As for me, this is my covenant with you. You will be the father of many nations….I will establish my covenant as an everlasting covenant between me and you and your descendants after you for the generations to come, to be your God and the God of your descendants after you. The whole land of Canaan, where you are now an alien, I will give as an everlasting possession to you and your descendants after you; and I will be their God"(Genesis 17:3, 7-8). Again, notice that there were no conditions attached to this. God was committing Himself to do this for Abraham. Period.

WITH ABRAHAM'S SON ISAAC

Isaac was the son of the covenant. God told Abraham and Sarah that they would have a son, even though Sarah was ninety and Abraham one hundred years old. Isaac was proof-positive that God kept His promises! Isaac inherited the responsibilities and wealth of his father and received this assurance from the Lord: "I will be with you and bless you. I will keep my promise to your father Abraham by giving this land to you and your descendants. I will give you as many descendants as there are stars in the sky, and I will give your descendants all of this land"(Genesis 26:3-4 CEV). The covenant remained intact and passed on from the father to the son.

Paul emphasized Isaac's place as the Covenant-Son in Galatians 4:28 in reminding us that we are free children of the Promise and not enslaved children condemned by the Law. The purpose of this covenant, he concludes, is that "it is for freedom that Christ has set us free. Stand firm, then, and do not let yourselves be burdened again by a yoke of slavery" (Galatians 5:1).

WITH ABRAHAM'S GRANDSON JACOB

Isaac was faithful to the God of his father, Abraham, and the Lord appeared to him and spoke with him. Jacob also encountered the Lord, though after a shaky start that included deceiving his father, exploiting his brother, and stealing from his father-in-law. He put all that behind him, however, after a life-changing experience with the Lord of Heaven (Genesis 32:22-30) and was faithful to the God of his father, Isaac. Later the Lord appeared to him, gave him a new name, and renewed the covenant. "I am God All-Powerful," said the Lord to Jacob, "and from now on your name will be Israel instead of Jacob. You will have many children. Your descendants will become nations and some of the men in your family will even be kings. I will give you the land that I promised Abraham and Isaac, and it will belong to your family forever" (Genesis 35:9-12 CEV). At this point, then, the same covenant—with no strings attached—had passed from father to son to grandson. Once again, God had declared that this was what HE was going to do.

Let's stop and remind ourselves once again about why God was doing this: why choose Abraham? Why choose Israel? Why bestow upon them a family and a people, land and a city, Jerusalem? Because He wanted to reveal Himself to the world and to undo the curse under which humanity had fallen. Israel would be His instrument or vehicle. Israel's leaders, kings, prophets and priests would be the means of bringing the Bible to the world at large. God would not only reveal Himself by speaking through nature and into the lives of His people but also by providing a written record of His dealings with His children. "What advantage, then, is there in being a Jew, or what value is there in circumcision?" asks the Apostle Paul in Romans 3, and answers, "Much in every way! First of all, they have been entrusted with the very words of God" (vs. 1-2).

It was God's plan that Israel would be a light to the nations of the world by responding to the Lord's love and mercy and grace. It was His plan that Jesus the Messiah would come into the world as a descendant of Abraham and that the land of Israel would be His place of birth (Isaiah 9:6-7; Micah 5:2). "God has clearly linked his name with Israel," comments one writer, "The authority of the Bible as God's Word can be put to the test through this everlasting covenant. God made this covenant with Abraham and his descendants so the people of the earth could see the authority of God's Word." He then quotes Numbers 6:27, "And they shall put my name upon the children of Israel; and I will bless them" and Deuteronomy 28:9-10, "If you follow and obey the Lord, he will make you his own special people, just as he promised. Then everyone on earth will know that you belong to the Lord, and they will be afraid of you" (CEV).

WITH DAVID

King David, one of Abraham's descendants, is described as "a man after God's own heart". God renewed the covenant with him. One day Nathan the prophet came to David with this word from the Lord: "David, this is what I, the Lord All-Powerful, say to you. I brought you in from the fields where you took care of sheep, and I made you a leader of my people....I have given my people Israel a land of their own where they can live in peace....Now I promise that like you your descendants will be kings. I'll choose one of your sons to be king when you reach the end of your life....I will be like a father to him, and he will be like a son to me. I will never put an end to my agreement with him...I will make sure that your son and his descendants will rule my people and my kingdom forever" (1 Chronicles 17:7-14 CEV).

WITH MOSES

About four hundred and fifty years after Abraham, the Lord made another covenant. It had to do with the giving of the Law to Moses. The Ten Commandments were a reflection of God's holiness and were part of the covenant. Bible scholars tell us that it was common at the time of Israel's deliverance from Egypt for kings and their subjects to enter into covenants. One type of covenant, called a "suzerainty" covenant, was a unilateral agreement made between a king and his vassal. The king issued a covenant within which the vassal found protection and security. But as the inferior party, the vassal was obligated to obey the conditions laid down by the king. One of the most striking aspects of the suzerainty covenant was the great emphasis placed on the king's care and compassion for his vassal. In turn the king expected the vassal to respond with gratitude for all that had been promised to him.[11]

Unlike the covenant with Abraham, this covenant was conditional but did not displace the Abrahamic covenant. The Ten Commandments were Israel's part of the suzerainty covenant given by God. If Israel were to enjoy all the privileges and blessings of having the Lord as her God, she would have to meet the requirements of the Law of Moses. "Now if you obey me fully and keep my covenant," said the Lord to Israel, "then out of all the nations you will be my treasured possession" (Exodus 19:5 NIV). It depended upon Israel whether she would abide by her part of the covenant and obey the Ten

---

[11] B.W. Anderson, *Understanding the Old Testament* (Englewood Cliffs, New Jersey: Prentice-Hall, Inc., 1966), p. 62.

Commandments and be blessed or break the covenant and be bereft of God's blessing.

ISRAEL SCATTERED AMONG THE NATIONS

Over and over again, the prophets warned the kings and priests of Israel that if they didn't keep the covenant the nation would be destroyed and the people scattered throughout the nations of the world. The message of the prophets was rejected and Israel paid the price of her rebellion: Israel was dispersed throughout the world. God's plan of redemption did not depend on Israel's obedience, but her potential for success as a nation did. Listen to the warnings of the prophets:

Deuteronomy 28:63-64 "The Lord is happy to make you successful and to help your nation grow while you conquer the land. But if you disobey him, he will be just as happy to pull you up by your roots. Those of you that survive will be scattered to every nation on earth...."(CEV)

Deuteronomy 30:1 "I have told you everything the Lord your God will do for you, and I've also told you the curses he will put on you if you reject him. He will scatter you in faraway countries" (CEV).

Leviticus 26:32-33 "Your land will become so desolate that even your enemies who settle there will be shocked when they see it. After I destroy your towns and ruin your land with war, I'll scatter you among the nations" (CEV).

After the reign of Solomon, the kingdom of Israel divided into two kingdoms: Israel to the north, consisting of ten tribes, and Judah to the south, consisting of two tribes. This made both kingdoms more vulnerable to powerful empires to the north and in 722 B.C. Israel was conquered by Assyria and its inhabitants deported. In 586 B.C. the southern kingdom, Judah, fell to the Babylonians and its people deported to Babylon.

Babylon, however, was conquered by the Persians in 539 B.C. and in the following year the Jews returned to Jerusalem, rebuilt the city, reconstructed the Temple, and under Ezra and Nehemiah restored government.

The next five hundred years were tumultuous ones for Israel. It fell to the Grecian Empire under Alexander the Great in the fourth century B.C. Such was the pressure from the Greek culture (or Hellenism) to subdue and root out Judaism during these years that the Jews revolted under Judah Maccabee, the leader of the rebellion, in 164 B.C. Jerusalem was liberated and a century of full political independence ensued. Alas, it all came to an end when Israel was swallowed up by the Roman Empire in 63 A.D. [12]

The great dispersion of the Jews throughout the world, however, didn't happen until 70 A.D., when the Roman army destroyed the nation of Israel, Jerusalem and the Temple, in putting down a massive Jewish rebellion. This dispersion lasted for almost 1900 years and ended in 1948 when Israel was once again recognized as a nation and became a member of the United Nations.

---

[12] *Carta's Historical Atlas.*

ISRAEL RESTORED

The prophets not only warned Israel that God would scatter them among the nations but also reminded them He would bring them back to the land and restore them as a nation. The dispersion throughout the world would be the means of bringing Israel back to God – something similar to Israel's experience in the wilderness for forty years preparing her to be the Lord's servant or instrument in the land of Canaan – and back to the land and nationhood. At the end of their wilderness journey, Moses spoke to the Israelites and said, "You are the Lord's people, because he led you through fiery trials and rescued you from Egypt" (Deut. 4:20 CEV). In Isaiah 48:10 we have a similar word from the Lord to Israel: "I, the Lord, am true to myself...I tested you in hard times just as silver is refined in a heated furnace. I did this because of who I am. I refuse to be dishonored or share my praise with any other god" (CEV).

Notice that prophet after prophet predicted a worldwide re-gathering of the scattered people of Israel:

Isaiah, prophesying about 750 B. C.: "In that day the Lord will reach out his hand a second time to reclaim the remnant that is left of his people from Assyria, from Lower Egypt, from Upper Egypt, from Cush, from Elam, from Babylonia, from Hamath and from the islands of the sea. He will raise a banner for the nations and gather the exiles of Israel; he will assemble the scattered people of Judah from the four quarters of the earth" (Isaiah 11:11-12). And again, "Do not be afraid, for I am with you; I will bring your children from the east and gather you from the west. I will say to the north, 'Give them up!' and to the south, 'Do not hold them back.' Bring my sons from afar and my daughters from the ends of the earth..." (Isaiah 43:5-6).

Finding a Firm Foundation in a Rapidly Changing World

Jeremiah prophesied around 600 B.C.: "I will bring them from the land of the north and gather them from the ends of the earth...They will come with weeping; they will pray as I bring them back. I will lead them beside streams of water on a level path where they will not stumble because I am Israel's father....He who scattered Israel will gather them and watch over his flock like a shepherd" (Jeremiah 31:8-10). A further word from Jeremiah is striking and amazing in its detail (after all this was written over 2600 years ago): "'the days are coming,' declares the Lord, 'when men will no longer say, 'As surely as the Lord lives, who brought the Israelites up out of Egypt,' but they will say, 'As surely as the Lord lives, who brought the Israelites up out of the land of the north and out of all the countries where he had banished them.' For I will restore them to the land I gave their forefathers" (Jeremiah 16:14-15)

Ezekiel prophesied at approximately 570 B.C.: He repeats the predictions that the Lord will bring back His people from the nations of the world to their land in chapter 36:19-24 and by doing so will demonstrate His holiness and sovereignty to the whole world. Then in chapter 37 we have Ezekiel's astonishing vision of the valley of dry bones – that rattle and shake and are refurbished with flesh and become a vast army: "Then he said to me: 'Son of man, these bones are the whole house of Israel. They say,'Our bones are dried up and our hope is gone; we are cut off.' Therefore prophesy and say to them.... 'This is what the Sovereign Lord says: 'I will take the Israelites out of the nations where they have gone. I will gather them from all around and bring them back into their own land. I will make them one nation in the land...they will never again be two nations or be divided into two kingdoms...for I will save them from their sinful backsliding, and I will cleanse them. They will be my people, and I will be their God....I will make a covenant of peace with them; it will be an everlasting covenant. I will establish them and increase their numbers, and I will put my sanctuary among them forever. My dwelling place will be with them; I will be their God, and they will be my people. Then the nations will know that I the Lord make Israel holy, when my sanctuary is among them forever" (vs.11, 21-23, 26-28).

What in Heaven's Name *has been* happening on earth? The God of Heaven has been making covenants with people on earth, and especially with His chosen people preparing them for that Day of all Days, for that Event of All Events, that Birth of All Births : God the Son born a human person, the Incarnation of the Holy One of Israel! The mind-boggling Covenant He came to provide is the subject of our next chapter.

SUGGESTED ORDER FOR SMALL GROUPS

APPROACHING WITH PRAISE AND WORSHIP

Choruses of prayers of praise, thanksgiving and adoration

PRAYER TIME

Prayers of confession, petition & intercession

BIBLE WARM-UP: The Old Testament Names of God

Finding a Firm Foundation in a Rapidly Changing World

El-Shaddai (el-shad-di): God Almighty or Almighty God, God the Omnipotent One. Trans. In the Bible as "Almighty God".

MEMORY VERSE

Genesis 50:20 *"You intended to harm me, but God intended it for good to accomplish what is now being done, the saving of many lives."*

DAILY BIBLE READINGS: WORDS & THOUGHTS FOR FURTHER REFLECTION

Day 1: Isaiah 12

_____
_____

Day 2: Isaiah 13

_____
_____

Day 3: Isaiah 14:1-17

_____
_____

What in Heaven's Name is Happening on Earth?

Day 4: Isaiah 12:18-32

_____

_____

Day 5: Isaiah 15

_____

_____

Day 6: Isaiah 16

_____

_____

Day 7: Isaiah 17

_____

_____

DISCUSSION QUESTIONS

1. What is the definition of "covenant"?

Finding a Firm Foundation in a Rapidly Changing World

2. What are some of the routine and special covenants or agreements that we all make in life? Discuss.

3. Read Genesis 8:21-22; 9:1-17. What did God say He would never do again? What was the sign He created and what was its significance?

4. Read Genesis 15:18; 17:3, 7-8 and compare with Exodus 19:5. What was the main difference between the covenant given to Abraham and the one given to Moses?

5. What is the common theme in the following Scriptures : Deuteronomy 28:63-64; 30:1; Leviticus 26:32-33? Discuss.

6. Find at least two Scriptures that predict the restoration of Israel to the land of Israel?

7. Read Romans 11:1-6, 11-24. How would you answer someone who told you that God was finished with Israel? What are these verses saying about the Lord's relationship to Israel and the Church?

CLOSING PRAYER: Gracious Holy Spirit, thank you for showing me my great need of the Lord Jesus and for giving me the faith to surrender my life to Him. Take my life and use me to bring glory to my Saviour and Lord. Thank you, Lord Jesus, for coming into the world and for coming into my life. Help me more and more to remove the obstacles in my life that hinder you from living through me. In Jesus' Name, I pray. Amen.

CHAPTER FOUR

A NEW COVENANT, A NEW HUMANITY

AND A NEW MEMORIAL

Adam was from the earth, and earthy, whereas the new body which Jesus now possesses is a fresh gift from heaven. The end result is the creation of a new type of human beings, once more in the image of God but now, more specifically, in the image of the risen Messiah: as we have born the image of the earthly human being, we shall also bear the image of the heavenly one.

N.T. Wright[13]

A NEW COVENANT

        A prominent theme of the Old Testament, if not the major theme, is that Israel wouldn't and couldn't keep her part in the covenant mediated by Moses on Mount Sinai. Paul argued in Romans 8:2-3 that the Mosaic covenant was

---

[13] *PAUL* (Minneapolis: Fortress Press, 2005), p. 28.

"powerless" because "it was weakened by the sinful nature". So God sent His own Son to live as a sinless human person and to be a "sin offering" for us "in order that the righteous requirements of the law might be fully met in us." In other words what was needed was a covenant that provided the means for God's children to be able to keep their part of the covenant. Forgiveness in the Old Testament was a gift for no more than a year based on the sacrifice of the best possible animal available, i.e., a lamb, a bullock, etc. All of this pointed forward to the time when God Himself would provide the ultimate Sacrifice: the Lord Jesus. John the Baptist pointed to Jesus and declared, "Look, the Lamb of God, who takes away the sin of the world!" (John 1:29). That's why the Bible tells us to "Thank God for his gift that is too wonderful for words" (2 Corinthians 9:15 CEV), referring to the Lord Jesus. To be saved, we simply accept the gift of Jesus' sinless life – that is, a life that was true to the covenant – and so inherit all the blessings of the covenant-keeping life that Israel and all of us found impossible to attain. In a nutshell, that's the astonishing message of the Gospel of Christ!

The replacing of the old covenant with a new and better one is the theme of Hebrews 8. The author of Hebrews stated that the New Covenant mediated by the Lord Jesus was superior to the old one mediated by Moses because "the covenant of which he is mediator…is founded on better promises"(vs. 6). He goes on to say that "by calling this covenant 'new,' he has made the first one obsolete" (vs. 13). This comparison 'between the Old and New Covenants spills over into chapter 9, in which it's revealed that the old order was a shadow of the eternal reality in the New Covenant mediated by the Lord Jesus: "The Holy Spirit was showing by this that the way into the Most Holy Place had not yet been disclosed as long as the first tabernacle was still standing" and that the Old Testament sacrifices and ceremonies were "only a matter of food and drink and various ceremonial washings – external regulations applying until the time of the new order" (vs.8-10).

FORETOLD BY PROPHETS

Towards the end of the Old Testament, this amazing message of God's love, mercy and grace began surfacing among the doom and gloom oracles of the prophets. Jeremiah and Ezekiel were the prophets of the New Covenant. "My eyes will watch over them for their good, and I will build them up and not tear them down; I will plant them and not uproot them," prophesied Jeremiah about the Babylonian exiles in words foreshadowing more elaborate future things, "I will give them a heart to know me, that I am the Lord. They will be my people and I will be their God, for they will return to me with all their heart"(Jeremiah 24:6-7).

In Jeremiah 31:31-33 the message couldn't be any clearer: "'The time is coming,' declares the Lord, 'when I will make a new covenant with the house of Israel and with the house of Judah. It will not be like the covenant I made with their forefathers when I took them by the hand to lead them out of Egypt, because they broke my covenant, though I was a husband to them,' declares the Lord. 'This is the covenant I will make with the house of Israel after that time,' declares the Lord. 'I will put my law in their minds and write it on their hearts. I will be their God, and they will be my people." One of the basic rules of interpreting the Bible is that the best interpretation of a passage of Scripture is when the Bible interprets itself. In Hebrews 8, after stating "if there had been nothing wrong with the first covenant, no place would have been sought for another" in verse 7, the author quotes this whole passage from Jeremiah 31 as proof of the New Covenant replacing the old one.

Ezekiel declares later on the same message even more strongly and with keener insight: "'This is what the Sovereign Lord says: Although I sent them far away among the nations and scattered them among the countries, yet for a little while I have been a sanctuary for them in the countries where they have gone….I will gather you from the nations and bring you back …and I will give you back the land of Israel again'. They will return to it and …. I will give them an undivided heart and put a new spirit in them ….Then they will follow my decrees and be careful to keep my laws" (11:17-20).

Again, the message is repeated in a slightly different way in Ezekiel 18:30-32 but sounding more and more like the New Testament: "Therefore, O house of Israel, I will judge you, each one according to his ways, declares the Sovereign Lord. Repent! Turn away from all your offenses; then sin will not be your downfall…get a new heart and a new spirit. Why will you die, O house of Israel? For I take no pleasure in the death of anyone, declares the Sovereign Lord. Repent and live!"

Ezekiel 36:25-27 reminds me even more of the New Testament message: "I will sprinkle clean water on you, and you will be clean; I will cleanse you from all your impurities and from all your idols. I will give you a new heart and put a new spirit in you; I will remove from you your heart of stone and give you a heart of flesh. And I will put my Spirit in you and move you to follow my decrees and be careful to keep my laws." Notice that in this passage there is absolutely no doubt about where our ability to keep the covenant would come from: "I will put my Spirit in you"!

THE NEW HUMANITY

Although the Lord Jesus repeatedly proclaimed and taught that He himself was the fulfillment of the momentous change or transformation in God's relationship with His children prophesied down through the centuries, His disciples didn't catch on until after the Day of Pentecost. They were so focused on the physical and material realm that their conception of the Lord Jesus was dominated by the conviction that He was the One, the Messiah, sent by God to get the Romans off their backs – someone very similar to what they read in their history books about Judah Maccabee, who freed Israel from the Greeks over a hundred years before. The suffering and bleeding Messiah prophesied in Isaiah 53 just wasn't on their radar at all – until the outpouring of the Holy Spirit on the Day of Pentecost, recorded in Acts 2. It took numerous appearances of the Risen and Living Lord to them and being filled with the Holy Spirit on Pentecost to remove their blindness - blindness to the fact that the Crucifixion was at the heart of God's Plan to restore and to deepen the loving relationship between the Creator and His children begun in the Garden of Eden. The Jews along with the disciples, believed in the coming of Messiah – they just couldn't grasp that Almighty God would come Himself in Person!

It was the same Peter who denied the Lord Jesus three times in Pilate's judgment hall, who stood up on the Day of Pentecost, newly filled with the Holy Spirit, who explained boldly to the multitude in Jerusalem that what they were witnessing had been prophesied in Joel 2:28-32 and that Jesus was the Chosen One of God. "This is how God fulfilled what he had foretold through all the prophets," preached Peter, "saying that his Christ would suffer. Repent, then, and turn to God, so that your sins may be wiped out, that times of refreshing may come from the Lord, and that he may send the Christ, who has been appointed for you – even Jesus. He must remain in heaven until the time comes for God to restore everything, as he promised long ago through his holy prophets" (Acts 3:18-21).

      Paul points out in more than one of his letters that what the Lord Jesus accomplished through His Crucifixion and Resurrection was nothing less than the creation of a new humanity. "We neither make nor save ourselves. God does both the making and saving. He creates each of us by Christ Jesus to join him in the work he does, the good work he has gotten ready for us to do, work we had better be doing…." wrote Paul to the formerly pagan Ephesian Christians. He continued: "You knew nothing of that rich history of God's covenants and promises in Israel, hadn't a clue about what God was doing in the world at large. Now because of Christ – dying that death, shedding that blood – you who were once out of it altogether are in on everything. The Messiah has made things up between us so that we're now together on this, both non-Jewish outsiders and Jewish insiders. He tore down the wall we used to keep each other at a distance. He repealed the law code that had become so clogged with fine print and footnotes that it hindered more than it helped. Then he started over. Instead of continuing with two groups of people separated by centuries of animosity and suspicion, he created a new kind of human being, a fresh start for everybody. Christ brought us together through his death on the Cross. The Cross got us to embrace, and that was the end of the hostility" (Ephesians 2:10-16 *The Message*).

The New English Bible translates Ephesians 2:14-16 in these words: "For he is himself our peace. Gentiles and Jews, he has made the two one, and in his own body of flesh and blood has broken down the enmity which stood like a dividing wall between them; for he annulled the law with its rules and regulations, so as to create out of the two a single new humanity in himself...."

THE NEW COVENANT MEMORIALIZED

As if to emphasize, it seems to me, that this New Covenant didn't in anyway change the Lord's promises and commitments to Israel, but rather was clear evidence that His plan for her was proceeding according to His purposes, the Lord Jesus made sure He celebrated the Passover Supper with His closest disciples the night before His arrest. He was a Jew and always would be. God's plan and purpose for Israel would proceed on a parallel track with His plan and purpose for the new humanity and, indeed, believing Israel would be included in it. Had He not promised that He would give Israel a new heart and a new spirit and put the Holy Spirit within her?

Out of the Passover Supper came the Lord's Supper (or Lord's Table memorial, Holy Communion, the Holy Eucharist or, in the Roman Catholic Church, the Mass). The Lord Jesus said to His disciples, "I have eagerly desired to eat this Passover with you before I suffer. For I tell you, I will not eat it again until it finds fulfillment in the kingdom of God....And he took bread, gave thanks and broke it, and gave it to them, saying, 'This is my body given for you; do this in remembrance of me.' In the same way, after the supper he took the cup, saying, 'This cup is the new covenant in my blood, which is poured out for you" (Luke 22:15-20).

Within a relatively short time, a short period of years, this memorial meal was happening in hundreds, perhaps thousands, of places throughout the Roman Empire. So much so that the Apostle Paul found it necessary to lay down some instructions as to how it should be properly and reverently celebrated in 1 Corinthians 11:17-34. Paul informs us that, among other purposes, one is to "proclaim the Lord's death until he comes" (vs. 26). It includes a backward and a forward look!

Shakespeare wrote what's "past is prologue."[14] We've looked at God's working among us in the past, in Part Two we turn to consider His work in the present: What in heaven's Name *IS* happening on Earth?

SUGGESTED ORDER FOR SMALL GROUPS

APPROACHING WITH PRAISE AND WORSHIP

Choruses or prayers of praise, thanksgiving & adoration

PRAYER TIME

Prayers of confession, petition & intercession

---

[14] *The Tempest,* Act 2, Scene 1.

Finding a Firm Foundation in a Rapidly Changing World

BIBLE WARM-UP: The Old Testament Names of God

Adonai (a-do-ni): the God who is Master, Lord, Owner of all that exists. Trans. In the Bible as "Lord".

MEMORY VERSE

Exodus 3:14 *"God said to Moses, 'I AM WHO I AM. This is what you are to say to the Israelites: "I AM has sent me to you."*

DAILY BIBLE READINGS: WORDS AND THOUGHTS FOR FURTHER REFLECTION

Day 1: Isaiah 18

_____

_____

Day 2: Isaiah 19

_____

_____

Day 3: Isaiah 20

_____

_____

Day 4: Isaiah 21

_____
_____

Day 5: Isaiah 22

_____
_____

Day 6: Isaiah 23

_____
_____

Day 7: Isaiah 24

_____
_____

DISCUSSION QUESTIONS

1. What was the weakness of the Old Testament Law according to Paul in Romans 8?

Finding a Firm Foundation in a Rapidly Changing World

2. How was sin dealt with in the Old Testament?

3. How is our sin handled differently under the New Covenant, according to John 1:29 and 1 John 1:7-9?

4. Read Jeremiah 31:31-33: Ezekiel 11:17-20; 18:30-32; 36:25-27. What is the theme of these passages and what makes them sound so much like the New Testament?

5. Discuss what it means to belong to "the new humanity" mentioned in Ephesians 2:10-16. (Read it in *The Message* in the Textbook)

6. What are the different names for Communion?

7. What do you think is the essential element in Communion, something without which it really wouldn't be Communion? See Luke 22:15-20; 1 Corinthians 11:17-34.

What in Heaven's Name is Happening on Earth?

CLOSING PRAYER: "Our Father, who art in heaven, hallowed be thy Name, thy kingdom come, thy will be done on earth as it is in heaven. Give us this day our daily bread and forgive us our trespasses, as we forgive those who trespass against us. And lead us not into temptation, but deliver us from the evil one. For thine is the kingdom, the power and the glory, forever and ever. Amen."

PART TWO

WHAT IN HEAVEN'S NAME *IS* HAPPENING ON EARTH?

What in Heaven's Name is Happening on Earth?

CHAPTER FIVE

THE LORD JESUS IS BUILDING HIS CHURCH!

Christianity is all about the belief that the living God, in fulfillment of his promises and as the climax of the story of Israel, has accomplished all this – the finding, the saving, the giving of new life – in Jesus. He has done it. With Jesus, God's rescue operation has been put into effect once and for all. A great door has swung open in the cosmos which can never again be shut.

N.T. Wright[15]

In Matthew 16:18 the Lord Jesus stated emphatically: "I will build my church, and the gates of Hades [or hell] will not overcome it [or "will not prevail against it" or "will not prove stronger than it"]. Whether we realize it or acknowledge it or not – because sometimes we get discouraged and see things

---

[15] *SIMPLY CHRISTIAN: Why Christianity Makes Sense* (New York: HarperOne Publishers, 2006), p.92.

What in Heaven's Name is Happening on Earth?

only from our own perspective or local situation – the Lord Jesus has been and is consistently and faithfully building His Church!

Don't be deceived: God is at work in our world and in our time!

THE HARVEST IS BEING REAPED!

The preaching of the Gospel and the planting of churches surged ahead after Pentecost, often in spite of harassment and persecution. The Christian faith spread throughout the Roman provinces, from one centre to another. In this work the Apostles and their co-workers did their essential part in laying the foundation, assisted by converted soldiers, sailors, slaves, merchants, landholders, men and women of every social class. In addition to the many European churches established by Paul in his missionary journeys, many important churches sprung up in Italy, on the Danube, the Rhine, in the Roman colonies. Also Gaul and Spain were evangelized, and it is probable that Paul visited the churches in Spain after his release from his first imprisonment in Rome. (It is not clear whether Paul was executed shortly after he reached Rome as recorded in Acts or was released and later re-arrested). By the middle of the second century, we know the Gospel had reached Asia because we have evidence of churches in Edessa, Mesopotamia, Persia,

Media, Armenia, and Arabia. Africa also was impacted in these early years of the Christian faith as we learn in Acts 8 of the Ethiopian treasurer's conversion on his way home from Jerusalem. Furthermore, early missionaries carried the Gospel all over Egypt from the great city of Alexandria, which became a strategic centre for the spread of Christianity.

Testimony both from Christians and non-Christians in Scripture and secular sources show that the converts to Christ multiplied with extraordinary speed in the first seventy years after Pentecost. The truth is that Christianity has never ceased to expand down through the centuries and right up to the present time. The Lord Jesus is building His Church and seems to be building it with increasing rapidity in our time.

Notice the following statistics compiled by reputable and well recognized researchers in the ministry of Missions:

In 2001, 178,356 people were added to the Church every day: for example, in Africa, 20,000; Latin America, 35,000; China, 28,000. This was a net gain of 44,000 churches yearly. In 2005, there were 1.9 billion Christians in the world, and today there are well over 2 billion. David A. Barret estimates that

What in Heaven's Name is Happening on Earth?

there will be 3 billion by 2025 if the current rate of growth continues.[16]

The number of Christians in Africa surged from 9.9 million in 1900 to 360 million in 2000, according to David Barret; and in Sub-Saharan Africa from 3% Christian in 1900 to 50% Christian in 1990.[17]

Latin America: in 1900, there were 50,000 believers; in 1980 that increased to 20,000,000; then in 1992, increased to 40,000,000; and in 2000, increased to 100,000,000. The change that has occurred in Latin America in a relatively few years has been nothing less than phenomenal. Dominated by Roman Catholicism for hundreds of years, everything has been changed by the rise of Pentecostalism. Beginning with a revival that broke out in a Methodist Church in Valparaiso, Chile, in 1909 "Latin American Pentecostalism has transformed the religious dynamic of the region," wrote Alister McGrath, longtime professor and theologian at Oxford University. "In Brazil, Chile, Guatemala, and Nicaragua, Pentecostals now far outnumber all other Protestant groups, and on some projections, they may soon constitute the majority of the population. Pentecostalism is also growing rapidly in areas adjacent to Latin America, such as the Caribbean, where Jamaica, Puerto Rico, and Haiti have seen large increases in Pentecostal congregations. These

---

[16] *U.S. Center for World Missions;* D.A.Barret, *World Christian Encyclopedia* (New York: Oxford Press,2001*), LINK,* p.west@mailbox.uq.edu.au.

[17] *World Christian Encyclopedia, p. 5;* Patrick Johnstone, *U.S Center for World Mission.*

developments, although noted in many research publications, have taken many in the West by surprise."[18]

Egypt: in 1996 the Egyptian Bible Society sold 3,000 video copies of the JESUS film; in 1997, in just a few weeks, 35,000 were sold at the Cairo International Book Fair; in 2000, 600,000 copies were sold; and in 2005 annual sales topped 750,000 copies of the Bible on audio-cassette, 200,000 to 300,000 full Bibles, and between 300,000 and 500,000 New Testaments.[19]

Morocco, Algeria, Sudan: Joel Rosenberg reports that when he visited Morocco in 2005 "Newspaper and magazine articles estimated that 25,000 to 40,000 Muslims have become followers of Jesus Christ in recent years." And in Algeria "in recent years" 80,000 have made commitments to the Lord Jesus, while in Sudan "more than one million Sudanese have turned to Christ just since the year 2000.[20]

South Korea: The Church has doubled from 6.1 million to 12.5 million in 6 years, 1986-1992. There are 7,000 churches in Seoul alone, including 9 of the largest in the world: 1986 there were 25,000 churches; 1992, increased to 37,000 churches. "Today Korea sends out Christian missionaries to nations throughout Asia, and increasingly to the large Korean diasporas of major Western cities, from Sydney to Los Angeles,

---

[18] Johnstone, *U.S. Center….;* Alister McGrath, *Christianity's Dangerous Idea,* (New York: HarperCollins, 2007), p. 450-451.

[19] Joel C. Rosenberg, *Epicenter* (Carol Stream, Illinois: Tyndale House, 2006), p.207.

[20] *Epicenter*, pp. 209-210.

What in Heaven's Name is Happening on Earth?

from Melbourne to New York..." observed Alister McGrath in *Christianity's Dangerous Idea.* "In 1979 Korean churches sent 93 missionaries overseas. In 1990 that number had increased to 1,645; in 2000 it stood at 8,103..South Korea is today home to some of the world's largest Protestant churches."[21]

Afghanistan: Before September 11, 2001, there were fewer than 100 known followers of Jesus in all of Afghanistan, states one report, but by 2008 Afghan Christian leaders were claiming more than 10,000 and that "Afghan Muslims are open to hearing the gospel like never before. Dozens of baptisms occur every week. People are snatching up Bibles and other Christian books as fast as they can be printed or brought into the country."[22]

Mongolia: in 1989 only 6 Christians; 1993 increased to 2,000; 1994 increased to 3000. In 1994 about 500 to 600 believers began a March for Jesus in fear and trembling but finished with rejoicing when they received help from the authorities.[23]

Myanmar: 37 of the top Buddhist monks in the nation converted to Christ at the premier showing of the "Jesus" film. Tribal peoples who have come to Christ are so hungry for the Bible and basic Christian teaching that they're trekking through

---

[21] *1992 Yearbook of the Korean Church*; A. McGrath, *Christianity's Dangerous Idea*, p. 448.

[22] J. Rosenberg, *Epicenter*, p. 211. See his *Inside the Revolution* (Carol Stream, Illinois: Tyndale House, 2009), p.400, for lower estimate of believers between 3,000 and 5,000.

[23] George Otis, Jr., *Sentinel Group*.

jungles and across mountains into Thailand in order to learn more about Jesus. They are doing this at great personal risk as intense persecution is widespread in Myanmar.[24]

Iran: Although the numbers can't be verified, Iranian Christian leaders report massive increases in converts to Christ. In 1979, the year of the Islamic Revolution, there were only about 500 known believers in Jesus, but by 2000 one survey of Christian demographic trends reported 220,000 Christians in Iran and between 4,000 and 20,000 were Muslim converts. Other claims are that by 2008 there were over a million or four million or almost seven million Christians in Iran. "In the last 20 years, more Iranians have come to Christ [than in] the last 14 centuries," stated an Iranian-born evangelist now based in Great Britain, "We've never seen such phenomenal thirst.... I believe this phenomenon [will] snowball into a major avalanche. This is still a rain. This is not the avalanche coming....But it will be happening very, very soon."[25]

The Lord Jesus has been building His Church unceasingly. No clearer proof of this is the following table:

The Ratio of Unbelievers to Believers[26]

A.D. 100 : 360 to 1	1900: 27 to 1	1990: 7 to 1
1000: 220 to 1	1950: 21 to 1	1994: 6.8 to 1
1500: 69 to 1	1980: 11 to 1	2000: 4 to 1

---

[24] *U.S. Center for World Mission.*

[25] Quoted in Rosenberg, *Inside the Revolution*, pp.384-385.

[26] *U.S. Center for World Mission.*

By 2010 the ratio was 3 to 1.

We are told in Matthew 24:14 that "when the good news about the kingdom has been preached all over the world and told to all nations, the end will come" (CEV). We are part of the first generation in the history of the world to have the technological ability to measure our progress in reaching that goal. What Paul started around 40 A.D., cross-culture missions, thousands of people on short-term missions now do every year. Between 1961 and 1991, there were three times the number of global evangelization plans than in the first 1500 years of Church history. About 200 years ago, only 100 people groups out of 12,000 had been reached with the Gospel; today only about 3000 remain. 70 % of all world evangelization has occurred since 1900. 70 % of that has been since World War Two. 70% of that has been in the last three years.[27]

Do your own figuring! With the wealth and technology that God has blessed us with and with over two billion people claiming to be Christian many understandably are thinking that it will not take long to fulfill Matthew 24:14 "This gospel of the kingdom will be preached in the whole world as a testimony to all nations, and then the end will come." Certainly, we are much closer that when we first believed!

THE LORD IS LOOKING FOR PARTNERS!

I want to show you and to persuade you – from the Bible – that the Lord earnestly desires and intends that you and

---

[27] Missions Report given at a Church conference, *"I Will Build My Church": Facts and Figures.*

I be actively involved in this wonderful harvest we've been discussing. The Lord is so pleased with us when we have a hands-on participation in bringing people to faith in Christ. In fact, He throws a Heavenly party, we're told, every time we succeed in harvesting one person (see Luke 15:7, 10). The Lord wants you and me to be His partner in ministry or His co-worker in reaping the harvest!

Right from the very beginning of His ministry, the Lord Jesus made it abundantly clear that His would not be a "Lone Ranger" type of ministry. It wasn't long before the Lord Jesus had chosen and called His Twelve Apostles (Mark 1:16-18).

Why did He choose them? The Gospels tell us and show us repeatedly that He was preparing them to work side-by-side with Him in proclaiming the Gospel by word and deed. We read in Luke 9:1-2 that "when Jesus had called the Twelve together, he gave them power and authority to drive out all demons and to cure diseases, and he sent them out to preach the kingdom of God and to heal the sick." Luke goes on to tell us that He equipped and sent out many more disciples: "After this the Lord appointed seventy-two [or seventy] others and sent them two by two ahead of him to every town and place where he was about to go. He told them, 'The harvest is plentiful, but the workers are few. Ask the Lord of the harvest, therefore, to send out workers into his harvest field. Go! I am sending you out like lambs among wolves….'" (Luke 10:1-3)

There is no indication at all from those verses that those He sent out were especially talented and naturally gifted. No! On the contrary, their only qualification seems to have been that they were followers or disciples of Jesus and were available. Am I a follower of the Lord Jesus? Are you a follower of Jesus? Yes! Then know without doubt that the Lord Jesus has sent us into the harvest as surely as He did the Twelve and the Seventy-Two and is delighted when we obey Him.

THE GOD WHO IS ALWAYS THERE!

All four Gospels, in their own unique way, conclude their account of our Lord's life by telling us that He will continue on working with us, side by side, in the Person of the Holy Spirit. Indeed, He told His disciples that that was the reason He had to return to Heaven – that the Holy Spirit would come so that He, the Lord Jesus, could live in each one of them. While on earth, He was confined to one human body; but back in Heaven He would be the God-who-knows-no-confinement once again and would take up residence in every person who accepted and embraced Him (see John 16:5-15). "If anyone does not have the Spirit of Christ," wrote the Apostle Paul, "he does not belong to Christ. But if Christ is in you …your spirit is alive… And if the Spirit of him who raised Jesus from the dead is living in you, he who raised Christ from the dead will also give life to your mortal bodies through his Spirit, who lives in you" (Romans 8:9-11).

Matthew 28:18-20 tells us that all authority "in heaven and on earth" was given to the Lord Jesus and, using that authority, He commands His followers to "go and make disciples of all nations, baptizing them in the name of the father and of the Son and of the Holy Spirit." He goes on to say – helping us to understand what a disciple of Jesus is supposed to do: "teaching them to obey everything I have commanded you" and what a disciple of Jesus is supposed to know: "and surely I am with you always, to the very end of the age."

Mark 16:15-20 informs us that the Good News is to be proclaimed to the whole "creation" and strikes an urgent note because those who do not believe will be "condemned". We are then told that all believers can count on miraculous happenings when they are engaged in this supremely important mission of bringing in God's harvest. Why? How? Because the Lord is our partner in all of this! With Him, nothing is impossible! "Then the disciples went out and preached everywhere, and the LORD WORKED WITH THEM and confirmed his word by the signs that accompanied it" (vs. 20. Emphasis added).

DON'T DO IT NOW, WAIT!

Luke, the physician, wrote the Gospel of Luke and the book of Acts. The books overlap with the last verses of Luke and the opening verses of Acts relating the last words of the Lord Jesus and his Ascension. Luke 24:46-49 repeats the Lord's command to take His message of repentance and forgiveness of sins to "all nations, beginning at Jerusalem." However, He instructs the disciples to stay in Jerusalem "until you have been clothed with power from on high." Acts 1:1-8 tells the same story just a little differently. These verses mention that the Lord Jesus ascended "after giving instructions through the Holy Spirit to the apostles he had chosen" and after assuring them that "you will receive power when the Holy Spirit comes on you; and you will be my witnesses in Jerusalem, and in all Judea and Samaria, and to the ends of the earth." In short, the Lord Jesus said, "Go and proclaim the Good News to all the nations" BUT don't do it now – WAIT until you've been filled with God the Holy Spirit! Ten days later it happened just as He said it would –

on the Day of Pentecost they were all filled with the Holy Spirit. And before the day was finished, they had harvested 3000 people! (Acts 2:1-4, 41)

What in Heaven's Name *IS* happening on Earth? God is bringing in His harvest and partnering joyfully with every child of His who rolls up his or her sleeves and pitches in!

SUGGESTED ORDER FOR SMALL GROUPS

APPROACHING WITH PRAISE AND WORSHIP

Choruses of prayers of praise, thanksgiving and adoration

PRAYER TIME

Prayers of confession, petition & intercession

BIBLE WARM-UP: The Old Testament Names of God

Jehovah-jireh (je-hov-ah yeereh): God our Provider.

MEMORY VERSE

Exodus 20:1-2 *"God spoke all these words: 'I am the LORD your God, who brought you out of Egypt, out of the land of slavery."*

Finding a Firm Foundation in a Rapidly Changing World

DAILY BIBLE READINGS: WORDS & THOUGHTS FOR FURTHER REFLECTION

Day 1: Isaiah 25

_____

_____

Day 2: Isaiah 26

_____

_____

Day 3: Isaiah 27

_____

_____

Day 4: Isaiah 28:1-15

_____

_____

Day 5: Isaiah 28:16-29

_____

_____

What in Heaven's Name is Happening on Earth?

Day 6: Isaiah 29:1-13

_____
_____

Day 7: Isaiah 29:14-24

_____
_____

DISCUSSION QUESTIONS

1. If we believed all that we hear on radio and TV, at work or at church, and what we read in newspapers and magazines, what picture of the Church or of Christians would we have? Discuss.

2. Why do you think we in North America and Europe are not seeing similar Spiritual Awakenings as in Korea, Latin America, etc.?

3.Discuss "The Ratio of Unbelievers to Believers" in the text. Read Matthew 24:14 and discuss what the implications of this might be.

4.Read Luke 15:7,10. Why does it surprise us that God can be happy and rejoice over someone or something? Or does it surprise you? Discuss.

5.The Lord Jesus commissioned His disciples in Luke 9:1-2 and 10:1-3. What do these commissions have in common?

6. Now read Mark 16:15-20. Would you agree that, taking these commissions together, we have a pretty good idea of what the Lord wants us to be up and doing?

7. Discuss the importance of "waiting" for the Holy Spirit in fulfilling the commission the Lord has given to us. See Luke 24:49 and Acts 1:8.

CLOSING PRAYER: Our Father, thank you for the gift of your Son, our Lord Jesus Christ, and for the great price you paid for my redemption. Thank you, Lord Jesus, for suffering on the Cross for me, paying the penalty for my sin and saving me. Thank you, Holy Spirit, for changing me and enabling me to love the Lord Jesus and to serve Him. Please come into my life in a greater and greater measure and make me a clean channel of the Father's love and grace. Thank you for choosing me to be your servant and your partner. I ask you to help me to serve you well and with my whole heart. In the Name of the Lord Jesus Christ, I pray. Amen.

Finding a Firm Foundation in a Rapidly Changing World

CHAPTER SIX

THE RESURRECTION OF AN OLD ENEMY

This has led some fervent supporters of Islam to regret that the Arabs were finally defeated and repulsed. What a wonderfully civilized empire would have been set up if all Europe had been invaded! This position, the opposite of the prevailing one in history up to about 1950, leads people to forget the horrors of Islam, the dreadful cruelty, the general use of torture, the slavery, and the absolute intolerance notwithstanding zealous apostles who underline Islam's toleration...It is enough to point out that wherever Islam gained a hold strong and vital churches like those of North Africa and Asia Minor simply disappeared. And all native cultures that were different, that the Romans and Germans had respected, were exterminated in areas conquered by the Arabs.

Jacques Ellul[28]

September 11, 2001, was a wake-up call for the whole world. Repeated announcements and news articles, television

---

[28] *THE SUBVERSION OF CHRISTIANITY* (Grand Rapids, Michigan: Eerdmans Publishing Company, 1986), p. 96.

What in Heaven's Name is Happening on Earth?

images constantly replaying the actual crash scenes with the Twin Towers in slow motion being destroyed before our eyes made it possible for billions of people around the world to hear that call. Even clearer than the Al-Qaeda message that the United States was a hated enemy because its troops were stationed in Islamic holy land and because it was the power behind Israel, was the message that humans can run but they cannot hide, no one is exempt from suffering and death, not even in the fabulously wealthy United States of America. 2,792 people died that terrible morning in the worst terrorist attack in U.S. history.

Two relevant questions: Why was the U.S. attacked? Why not London, Paris, Brussels, Berlin or Moscow? After all, although a powerful superpower, the U.S. has been wonderfully generous and kind to many nations, some that could contribute little to U.S. self-interest. Gordon Sinclair, a Canadian journalist, writer and commentator, felt it necessary in June 1973 to speak up for the U.S. in a radio editorial , words that reverberated and resonated throughout the media at that time. Again, as in 1973, his message struck responsive chords in the aftermath of nine/eleven. The following is an edited version:

"This Canadian thinks it is time to speak up for the Americans as the most generous and possibly the least appreciated people on all the earth. Germany, Japan and, to a lesser extent, Britain and Italy were lifted out of the debris of war by the Americans who poured in billions of dollars and forgave other billions in debts.

None of these countries is today paying even the interest on its remaining debts to the United States. When

Finding a Firm Foundation in a Rapidly Changing World

France was in danger of collapsing in 1956, it was the Americans who propped it up, and their reward was to be insulted and swindled on the streets of Paris. I was there. I saw it.

When earthquakes hit distant cities, it is the United States that hurries in to help. This spring, 59 American communities were flattened by tornadoes. Nobody helped. The Marshall Plan and the Truman Policy pumped billions of dollars into discouraged countries. Now newspapers in those countries are writing about the decadent, war mongering Americans.

You talk about Japanese technocracy, and you get radios. You talk about German technocracy, and you get automobiles. You talk about American technocracy, and you find men on the moon – not once, but several times – and safely home again.

You talk about scandals, and the Americans put theirs right in the store window for everybody to look at. Even their draft-dodgers are not pursued and hounded. They are here on our streets, and most of them, unless they are breaking Canadian laws, are getting American dollars from ma and pa at home to spend here.

When the railways of France, Germany and India were breaking down through age, it was the Americans who rebuilt them. When the Pennsylvania Railroad and the New York Central went broke, nobody loaned them an old caboose. Both are still broke.

I can name you 5000 times when the Americans raced to the help of other people in trouble. Can you name me even one time when someone else raced to the Americans in trouble? I don't think there was outside help even during the San Francisco earthquake.

Our neighbors have faced it alone, and I'm one Canadian who is damned tired of hearing them get kicked around. They will come out of this thing with their flag high. And when they do, they are entitled to thumb their nose at the lands that are gloating over their present troubles. I hope Canada is not one of those."[29]

Whether or not you share the sentiment expressed by Gordon Sinclair, it highlights the question that still remains of why New York and why the widespread anti-Americanism, even in Canada and Britain, when the U.S. took and is taking action against the Islamic terrorists? It is so virulent and nasty that, it seems to me, it is something more than the usual negative ethnic prejudice.

ANTI-AMERICANISM

I'm wondering and suggest to you that this anti-Americanism – that was seen clearly in our government in Canada abandoning traditional alliances and supporting the blatant anti-Americanism of France and Germany in the United Nations Security Council in the period immediately following nine/eleven – is even more demonic than the usual ethnic prejudices. Could it be that the United States is paying the price

---

[29] Originally written for a Toronto newspaper and entitled "The Americans," it was broadcast over radiio on June 5, 1973. (www.truthorfiction.com/gordonsinclair.htm).

of unstinted support for Israel, the nation described in the Bible as "the apple of God's eye" and the people whom Satan has been trying to destroy from birth?

Why should Satan be so enraged against Israel? Because she was and is the "mother" of the Messiah, the incarnate God the Son. This is the clear message of the vision in Revelation 12:1-6, 13-17:

> "A great and wondrous sign appeared in heaven a woman clothed with the sun, with the moon under her feet and a crown of twelve stars on her head [Israel]. She was pregnant and cried out in pain as she was about to give birth. Then another sign appeared in heaven: an enormous red dragon with seven heads and ten horns and seven crowns on his heads. His tail swept a third of the stars out of the sky and flung them to the earth. The dragon stood in front of the woman who was about to give birth, so that he might devour her child the moment it was born. She gave birth to a son, a male child, who will rule all the nations with an iron scepter [the Lord Jesus]. And her child was snatched up to God and to his throne. The woman fled into the desert to a place prepared for her by God….the great dragon was hurled down – that ancient serpent called the devil, or Satan, who leads the whole world astray. He was hurled to the earth, and his angels with him….
>
> When the dragon saw that he had been hurled to the earth, he pursued the woman who had given birth to the male child….Then the dragon was enraged at the woman and went off to make war against the rest of

her offspring – those who obey God's commandments and hold to the testimony of Jesus [Christians who are devout followers of the Lord Jesus]."

Why the U.S.? Could it be that the U.S. is the focus of evil, of Satan, at this time because of its support and championing of Israel, the woman of Revelation 12?. Indeed, the U.S. is like two wings of an eagle to Israel and literally so when we think of the magnificent Israeli Air Force - provided by the U.S. and the bulwark of Israel's defense. The goal, at this time, is to destroy Israel; the U.S. is only of secondary importance – and that brings us to the second question: Why now?

The U. S. has been a staunch supporter of Israel for decades, right back to its struggle for survival after its rebirth in 1948 when millions of Arabs surrounded her and sought to strangle her in infancy. So why attack the U.S. at this particular time?

Two further reasons come to mind in addition to its support of Israel. One is the world-wide expansion of the U.S. culture. Although there is much that is good and helpful and life-enhancing in U.S. exports, for example, technology, manufactured goods, foods, etc., there is also a great amount of smut and garbage that is offensive to religious people of every receiving nation. Included in this are pornography, immorality and violence that spews out of Hollywood. This is immediately pounced upon by Islamic leaders and denounced as the natural fruit of America's Christian religion and democracy. As the Ayatollah Khomeini of Iran told the world so often, the U.S. was the Great Satan and U.S. society a cesspool of filth. And that leads to the second reason: the historic hostility between Islam and Christianity and in recent years the rise of Islamic terrorists.

THE RISE OF ISLAM

What do we know about Islam? Increasingly it is being exposed to the whole world and we would do well to pay attention to its origins, beliefs and ultimate goals. It is worth remembering that an Islamic empire followed the Roman Empire and dominated the world for hundreds of years.

It began with Muhammad, a caravan leader who was very familiar with both Jews and Christians. He began getting his own words and revelations about god in A.D. 610, the year the Quran (Koran) revelations began. Muhammad believed the angel Gabriel spoke to him when he was meditating in a cave near Mecca. He claimed these were the words of the one true god, Allah. These words were written down over a period of about 22 years. It's important to know that these words were not the teachings of Muhammad, but the words of Allah. The life and teachings of Muhammad are found in another set of Islamic holy writings called the books of Hadith. It is interesting to note that at the beginning of Islam, its leader tried to persuade both Jews and Christians to endorse his new revelations about the true god.[30]

At the beginning of his revelations, in Mecca, Muhammad (570-632) focused on converting worshippers of idols and, probably because he lacked military means, no form

---

[30] R.F. Safa, *Inside Islam* (Lake Mary, Florida: Charisma House, 1996), pp.24-27.

of compulsion was used. That lasted for the first ten to twelve years. But that changed when he moved to Medina in the early 620s – then Islam became political as well as religious and spiritual. Indeed this migration began on September 24, 622, and this is the date that marks the beginning of the Muslim calendar. Shortly after his move to Medina, he believed he had received a new revelation to fight against all those who "believe not in Allah…and those who acknowledge not the religion of truth (i.e. Islam) among the people of the Scripture (Jews and Christians)…."[31]

One scholar, a former Muslim and professor of Islamic history in Egypt, Mark Gabriel, writes that there are five key requirements that must be met in order to be a Muslim. These requirements are known as the five "pillars of Islam":

1. Statement of belief. "There is no god but Allah, and Muhammad is his prophet."
2. Prayer – five times a day while facing Mecca, the birthplace of Muhammad: at dawn, afternoon, late afternoon, after sunset and night. Special prayers on Fridays.
3. Giving alms. It is like a tax and is paid at the end of the year and given to those in need.
4. Fasting. This occurs during the Islamic month of Ramadan, which begins in the middle of November. No eating or drinking during daylight hours but light eating and drinking before sunrise and a more substantial meal after sunset.

---

[31] M. Gabriel, *Islam and Terrorism* (Mary Lake, Florida: Charisma House, 2002), p.73.

> 5. Pilgrimage. Every Muslim is encouraged to make a pilgrimage at least once in life to Mecca, and to participate in the five-day ritual that is followed.[32]

Islam is a religion based on works and there is no guarantee of Paradise. Only Allah knows and decides that. "Then as for him whose balance (of good deeds) will be heavy, he will live a pleasant life (in Paradise). But as for him whose balance (of good deeds) will be light, he will have his home in *Hawiyah* (pit, i.e., hell)" (Surah 101:6-9, *The Noble Quran*). The only way to know for certain about going to Paradise is to die in *jihad*, i.e., to die while fighting the enemy of Islam. No wonder the Palestinian terrorists and Al-Qaeda succeeded in attracting suicide bombers and extremists. This helps us also to understand why Muslims will leave their own country to fight jihad in other countries: it is the only way a Muslim can be assured of entering Paradise.[33]

MORE ABOUT MUHAMMAD

Muhammad was born in the year 570 in the Arabian Desert. His father died before he was born and life in the Desert being hard at the best of times, his mother returned home with her baby to live with her family. She died when he

---

[32] Mark Gabriel, *Islam and Terrorism*, pp.26- 28.

[33] *Ibid.* See also Brigitte Gabriel, *They Must Be Stopped : Why We Must Defeat Radical Islam and How We Can Do It* (New York: St. Martin's Press, 2008), pp.18-23.

was only six years old and his paternal grandfather became his guardian. But within a short time his grandfather died.

His time with his grandfather, however, was a highly impressionable period of his life and impacted him spiritually. His grandfather was the caretaker of Al-Kaaba, the centre of idol worship in Mecca. Muhammad would have inside exposure to the idol worship of the time. People came from all over Arabia to worship there and each tribe had its own idol in the temple. When his grandfather died, his uncle took over his responsibilities in Al-Kaaba and also took over the care of Muhammad. He was a frequent visitor to Al-Kaaba and witnessed "the people bowing down to these statues, and he saw the businessmen who made a living by making and selling the statues." It seems, however, he was repulsed by it all and vowed that "when he grew up he would never bow down to one of the idols that existed throughout Mecca and Arabia at that time." [34]

At a young age he began tending sheep. His uncle was also in business as a caravan trader and began taking Muhammad with him. On a trip to Syria he met a Nestorian priest (a popular cult in Syria, the Nestorians came out of Christianity because they denied the Trinity and the divinity of Jesus). The priest noticed a little birthmark on the boy's shoulder and told this uncle that "this child is going to be the final prophet for our world. This is the stamp of prophethood." Then he warned them not to let the Jews see the birthmark as they would try to kill him. The warning left its mark on

---

[34] M. Gabriel, *Islam and the Jews* (Mary Lake, Florida: Charisma House, 2003), p. 73.

Muhammad and influenced his later relationships with the Jewish communities in Arabia.

Muhammad eventually became a caravan leader and led camel caravans to exchange goods in places like Syria and Yemen. The caravan he led was owned by the wealthiest and most powerful woman in the area. They later married, when he was twenty-five and she was over forty and had children. Her name was Khadija.

Fifteen years later, Muhammad had the first of his revelations. He believed that the angel Gabriel had appeared to him while he was meditating in a cave. This was the beginning of Islam. Was this being the angel Gabriel? Is Allah the God of the Bible? Mark Gabriel clearly rejects these claims and dismisses Muhammad's revelations , but states that. "the name *Allah* was used in pre-Islam Arabia to refer to one of the 360 idols in Kaaba. Allah was supposed to be the greatest god. Some tribes used the name to refer to the moon god." [35]

ISLAM AND TERRORISM

The ultimate goal of Islam, states Mark Gabriel, "is to establish Islamic authority over the whole world. Islam is not just a religion; it is a government, too. That is why it always gets down to politics. Islam teaches that Allah is the only authority; therefore, political systems must be based on Allah's teaching and nothing else." Therefore, jihad is only successful when a nation declares Islam as its religion and as its government! There are a few examples of this: Afghanistan under the

---

[35] *Ibid*.

What in Heaven's Name is Happening on Earth?

Taliban, Iran and Sudan. It is helpful to understand that not even the "secular" Muslim nations escape the potential violence of the Islamic terrorists, such nations as Algeria, Egypt, Syria, Turkey, Palestine, Iraq, Lebanon, Saudi Arabia, Libya, Malaysia and others. The Islamic fundamentalists want to overthrow these governments and bring in a full-blown Islamic revolution.[36] Indeed this is what happened and is happening in what is being called "The Arab Spring." Already Tunisia, Yemen, Egypt, Gaza and Libya have been revolutionized and, even as I write (September, 2012), Syria is on the brink of falling.

So does that mean that every Muslim is out to overthrow our democratic governments? Mark Gabriel points out that there are different kinds of Muslims just as there are different kinds of Christians. He goes on to state that there are mainly three groups of Muslims:

1. There are secular Muslims. They are the ones who accept the non-violent parts of Islam but reject the call to jihad. This would be true of the majority of Muslims around the world. They accept and practice the cultural aspects of Islam but are not truly representing Islam

2. There are traditional Muslims. Two types: the first includes people who study Islam, know it and practice it, but they struggle with the concept of jihad and consider it to refer to spiritual warfare and not physical. The second type are those who know what jihad is about but do not take action because (a) they do not have the ability to do it by themselves, (b) they are concerned about what would happen to their lives, family

---

[36] M. Gabriel, *Islam and Terrorism*, p.37-38.

and children if they join a fundamentalist group, or (c) they want to live a comfortable life on earth without fear of dying.

3. There are fundamentalist Muslims. These are the terrorists. Their aim is to practice Islam as Muhammad did. Though we call them extremists, they are practicing true Islam. The goal of the fundamentalists, of course, is to stir up the "secular" and "traditional" Muslims to join them in the jihad against, first of all, Israel, and then any and all non-Islamic nations. They believe Allah destined them to rule the world, and we often forget that Islam ruled the world for centuries. As Gabriel comments, it is nothing like what is described in the media, which he describes as either wishful thinking or downright "deceit with intent to attract converts." [37]

In conclusion, we should take note of perhaps another reason why it seems all hell has broken loose over the past few years. Revelation 12:10-12 exhorts the followers of the Lord Jesus to rejoice and be glad because the "enormous red dragon," "the ancient serpent called the devil, or Satan" has been defeated and those who love and serve the Lord Jesus have "overcome him by the blood of the Lamb and by the word of their testimony," and by their love of Jesus to the death. Then there follows this warning: "But woe to the earth and the sea, because the devil has gone down to you! He is filled with fury, because he knows that his time is short." Have we entered or are entering that period when the devil "knows that his time is short"?

---

[37] *Ibid.*, pp.38-39.

What in Heaven's Name is Happening on Earth?

SUGGESTED ORDER FOR SMALL GROUPS

APPROACHING WITH PRAISE AND WORSHIP

Choruses of prayers of praise, thanksgiving and adoration

PRAYER TIME

Prayers of confession, petition & intercession

BIBLE WARM-UP: The Old Testament Names of God

Jehovah-rophe (je-ho-vah ro-phay): God our Healer.

MEMORY VERSE

Deuteronomy 6:4-5 *"Hear, O Israel: The LORD our God, the LORD is one. Love the LORD your God with all your heart and with all your soul and with all your strength."*

DAILY BIBLE READINGS: WORDS & THOUGHTS FOR FURTHER REFLECTION

Finding a Firm Foundation in a Rapidly Changing World

Day 1: Isaiah 30:1-14

_____
_____

Day 2: Isaiah 30:15-33

_____
_____

Day 3: Isaiah 31

_____
_____

Day 4: Isaiah 32

_____
_____

Day 5: Isaiah33

_____
_____

Day 6: Isaiah 34

What in Heaven's Name is Happening on Earth?

_____
_____

Day 7: Isaiah 35

_____
_____

DISCUSSION QUESTIONS

1. Where were you on 9/11?

2. Discuss why you think the terrorists chose the U.S. and not Russia, Germany, France or Britain.

3. Read Deuteronomy 32:9-10 and Zechariah 2:7-9. Do you think that the U.S. might be under attack because her support for Israel has enraged Satan against her? Or, as some point out, that it might be because the U.S. is pressuring Israel to give up land God gave to Israel and called it "my land"?

4. Discuss the vision in Revelation 12. What do you make of it? What is clear and what is puzzling?

5. What are the five "pillars" of Islam? Discuss

6. What are the three groups of Muslims? Discuss ways and means we can befriend and love Muslims and share our faith with them.

7. Do you think that Revelation 12:10-12 might be upon us and that we've entered the period when the devil "knows that his time is short"?

CLOSING PRAYER: Lord Jesus, we bow before you alone because you are King of Kings and Lord of Lords. You alone are worthy of our worship and praise and adoration. Thank you that you are mighty to save and to deliver and thank you for saving and delivering us. Help us to be determined to love and serve you always, and by your grace to be strong in you and in your mighty power. Holy Spirit, fill us and use us to bring deliverance to the captives and healing to the sick and comfort to the afflicted. Help us to follow in your steps, Lord Jesus. We ask this in your Strong and Mighty Name, Amen.

What in Heaven's Name is Happening on Earth?

Finding a Firm Foundation in a Rapidly Changing World

CHAPTER SEVEN
ISRAEL'S SURVIVAL AND WORLDWIDE ISLAMIC EXPANSION

Mutual hostility between Israel and Iran has burned hot ever since Iran's Islamic Revolution of 1979. But rarely, if ever, has the prospect of outright war between the two countries been as real as it is now.....Iranian President Mahmoud Ahmadinejad is doing little to calm Israeli fears about Iranian intentions. In an August speech to mark al-Quds Day – an annual event begun in Iran in 1979 to show solidarity with Palestinians and to protest Israeli control of Jerusalem – Ahmadinejad told a rally in Tehran that 'the Zionist regime and the Zionists are a cancerous tumour' and warned against 'one cell of them' being left in Palestinian land in the future. The nations of the region, he added, will 'soon finish off the usurper Zionists in the Palestinian land,' and a new Middle East will emerge with no trace of either Americans or Zionists.

Michael Petrou[38]

Anyone who daily reads the newspapers, listens to news reports and keeps up with what is happening on the international scene – and has done so over the years – can't

---

[38] "War now? Or war later?" *MACLEAN'S MAGAZINE*, Oct. 15, 2012, p. 50.

What in Heaven's Name is Happening on Earth?

help but wonder why the little sliver of land called Israel dominates the headlines throughout the world. An article by Michael Coren, columnist and television personality, in *The Calgary Sun, August 23, 2003* ran with the headline "Lazy criticism targets Israel" and sub-title "Left-wing media blames tiny strip of land for almost all world's evils". The author, obviously sympathetic to Israel, bemoans the poor press Israel inevitably receives even though the "country has been in existence for a little over 50 years, and in that time, has introduced concepts of democracy, civil rights, pluralism, religious freedom, gender equality, the rule of law, the separation of powers, a free press and the right to protest ." The point he is making here, of course, is that Israel is no different than the other secular and democratic nations, and even more secular than some.

Coren goes on to observe that the press currently is complaining that Israel limits the freedom of movement in combat zones and sensitive areas. "There is, indeed, a slight limitation now, after so many suicide bombings and so much biased reporting. But the limits are minor. In comparison to any Arab state, Israel allows foreign reporters absolute freedom. Why so little complaint about this? Yet, if we read many newspapers and listen to so much television and radio, this tiny strip of land in an ocean of dictatorship, murderous oligarchy and religious despotism, is responsible for almost every evil in the world, including baldness, bad breath and the rain." Obviously, a little exaggeration in that last phrase – but just a little! Fifteen years ago Barbara Amiel, another Canadian journalist, made the same point in a MACLEAN'S magazine article entitled, "In need of another small miracle." She wrote, "We don't bother asking the questions anymore. These days most news is bad news for the Jews as every newspaper features photos of tough-looking Israeli soldiers confronting cowering Palestinian women and children." Nothing, it seems, has changed!

Michael Coren goes on to address the constant clamour of the media for the land to be "returned" to the Palestinians as the rightful owners. "If only these shock hacks knew their history. The Jewish people never left Israel, even though the majority were driven out by the Romans, a genuinely cruel colonial power. Many managed to stay, and simply because Arab and Islamic imperialists eventually conquered the near east and Israel – does not make this [Israel] an Arab land....I always find it ironic that the hysterical left, self-loathing Jews and anti-Semites scream about Zionism [the organized movement of Jews going back to Israel], when all the Jews are doing is taking back what always belonged to them in the first place."

Coren acknowledges that not all critics of Israel are anti-Semitic but wonders why "they are not more angry at any of the numerous Latin American, African or Asian states that murder, torture and rape." He puts it down to "at the very least lazy and selective criticism." He concludes by putting his finger on the whole nub of the problem: "There are valid objections to be made of some Israeli actions and of some Israeli leaders. But if the Arab world would affirm *the absolute right to existence of the Jewish state* in a sea of increasingly violent and paranoid Islam, most of these problems could be dealt with."

ISLAM'S HOLY LAND

What in Heaven's Name is Happening on Earth?

According to Mark Gabriel, in his book *Islam and the Jews*, that is just not going to happen because Islam believes and teaches that Israel is occupying Islamic holy land. In other words, in order for the Arab states to recognize Israel's right to the land, they would have to reject a primary teaching of their own religion. Gabriel points to those leaders who have moved towards recognizing Israel's right to exist, like Anwar Sadat, President of Egypt, have been assassinated by their own people. That doesn't give an awful lot of incentive to Arab leaders to embrace Israel's right to exist!

Quoting from the Quran, Osama bin Laden and other Islamic authorities, Gabriel states that there are "two key beliefs that keep Muslims in never-ending conflict with the state of Israel. They are: (1)a belief that the land belongs to Islam and (2) a belief that the holy mosque in Jerusalem must be kept pure." The inevitable result of these beliefs, he argues, is that "No peace negotiation is acceptable" and "Israel as a nation must be destroyed." One startling quotation is used by him to justify this point of view from a publication by the Islamic Assembly of North America. Written by a Muslim scholar, the booklet *No for Normalization* is absolutely uncompromising: "The Jews came and attacked this land and stole it, and this will not change the fact that this land is Muslim, and it will remain that way forever. If we aren't able to liberate this land today from the Jews, this doesn't mean that we can give it up. We have to work until the time comes, and then we will bring it back to the Islamic world." This was published by Muslims living in North America in 2000. (There are between 6 and 8 million Muslims in the U.S.)[39]

---

[39] M Gabriel, *Islam and the Jews*, p. 86.

Finding a Firm Foundation in a Rapidly Changing World

In an unsettling chapter in his book *Islam and Terrorism*, Gabriel deals with "The Three Stages of Jihad." The three stages historically have been: (1) Weakened Stage (2) Preparation Stage, and (3) Jihad Stage.

The Weakened Stage is when Muslims are a small, weak minority living in a non-Muslim society. This is not a time to dwell on jihad but to live quietly and lawfully and work to increase Islamic converts and attract Muslims from other places. Pointing out that the media often uses verses from the Quran to describe this as the natural and correct depiction of Islam, he contends that these verses were written when Islam was in its infancy and in a weak and vulnerable condition. "After his movement gained strength, Muhammad received new words that cancelled out (*nasikh*) these verses." Apparently, *nasikh* is the word used for the process of a later revelation canceling out a previous one and has been used many times in justifying Muslim political and military actions.

The Preparation Stage happens when the Muslim community is a reasonably influential minority. "Because their future goal is direct confrontation with the enemy, they make preparations in every possible area – financial, physical, military, mental and any other area." He then quotes from the Quran: "Let not Unbelievers think that they can get the better (of the godly); they will never frustrate (them). *Against them make ready your strength to the utmost of your power,* including steeds of war, to strike terror into (the hearts of) the enemies, of Allah and your enemies, and others besides whom you may not know, but whom Allah knows." There follows an interesting and telling modern commentary by Islamic scholarship, like our Bible commentaries, on the italics portion of that quote: "And make ready against them all you can of power, including steeds of war (*tanks, planes, missiles, artillery*) to threaten the enemy of Allah..." Gabriel concludes that "this commentary should confirm for the reader that Muslims are practicing this verse in modern times."

The Jihad Stage is when the Muslim community is influential and powerful: At this stage every Muslim's duty is to actively fight the enemy, overturning the system of the non-Muslim country and establishing Islamic authority. Mark Gabriel substantiates this with a Quran quote from Muhammad's last revelation from Allah, when Islam was established and strong: "Fight and slay the Pagans wherever you find them, and seize them, beleaguer them, and lie in wait for them in every stratagem (of war)..."

This former Muslim and professor of Islamic Studies at an Islamic University, concludes the chapter with the statement: "Muslims are commanded to kill anyone who chooses not to convert to Islam. The verse says 'wherever you find them.' There are no geographical limits." He then refers to Muhammad's own example at Mecca and Medina and the modern example of Lebanon encompassing the three stages.[40]

NINE/ELEVEN

Nine/eleven, of course, wasn't the first experience the United States had of Islamic radicals. Islamic extremists had already been on the scene before September 11, 2001. There

---

[40] Gabriel, *Islam and Terrorism*, (Mary Lake, Fl.: Charisma House, 2002), pp. 85-87; see also Brigitte Gabriel, *They Must Be Stopped*, for an eyewitness account of Islam in Lebanon.

was the bombing of the Marine Barracks in Lebanon in the 1980s; the bombing of the World Trade Center in 1993; the bombing of the U.S. embassies in Africa ; and the attack on the U.S.S. Cole in 2000 off the coast of Yemen.

Since nine/eleven there has been the on-going war against terrorism in Afghanistan, Iraq and wherever al Qaeda strongholds could be found. Worldwide news headlines of that war have been the execution of Saddam Hussein and the assassination of Osama bin Laden. But the war against Islamic terrorism continues unabated and, some would argue, it has not diminished. If anything has changed, it is how the terrorists have adapted to the new situations in Afghanistan and Iraq and continue to terrorize the world.

THE ARAB SPRING

The Arab Spring refers to democratic revolutions that have occurred or are occurring in Arab nations. Islam has found and is finding that the most effective way to Islamize the world is by democratic elections. So far that's what the Arab Spring is all about. In Tunisia, Egypt (representing one-third of the entire Arab world population), Bahrain, Yemen, Morocco, it is the Muslim Brotherhood that has emerged victorious and the best organized party in each election. What is the Muslim Brotherhood? The first of the modern Islamic terrorist organizations, the oldest and most sophisticated, out of which came seventy offshoot organizations around the world, including al Qaeda and Hamas. [41] The Muslim Brotherhood was

---

[41] R. Spencer, *Religion of Peace? Why Christianity Is and Islam Isn't* (Washington, D.C.: Regnery Publishing,Inc., 2007), pp. 140-141.

responsible for the assassination of Anwar Sadat of Egypt because he signed the peace treaty with Israel. Its anthem or motto is "Allah is our objective. The Prophet is our leader. Qur'an is our law. Jihad is our way. Dying in the way of Allah is our highest hope."[42]

Brigitte Gabriel, who keeps a keen watch on Islamic activities within the U.S., points to a document conceived by the Muslim Brotherhood detailing plans for the next hundred years that was found in Switzerland in November 2001, shortly after nine/eleven. The plan is about radical Islam infiltrating and dominating the West in order to establish an Islamic government on earth. In counterterrorism circles this document has become known as "The Project." The document consists of fourteen pages, written in Arabic, and contains tactics and plans for establishing Islam throughout the world. Here is a sample:

- Networking and coordinating actions between like-minded Islamist organizations.

- Avoiding open alliances with known terrorist organizations and individuals to maintain the appearance of "moderation."

- Infiltrating and taking over existing Muslim organizations to realign them toward the Muslim Brotherhood's collective goals.

---

[42] B. Gabriel, pp. 73-74.n

- Using deception to mask the intended goals of Islamist actions, as long as it doesn't conflict with Sharia law.

- Avoiding social conflicts with Westerns locally, nationally, or globally that might damage the long-term ability to expand the Islamist power base in the West or provoke a backlash against Muslims.

- Putting into place a watchdog system for monitoring Western media to warn Muslims of international plots fomented against them.

- Developing a comprehensive hundred-year plan to advance Islamist ideology throughout the world.

- Instrumentally using existing Western institutions until they can be converted and put into the service of Islam.

- Instituting alliances with Western "progressive" organizations that share similar goals.

- Making the Palestinian cause a global wedge issue for Muslims.

- Adopting the goals of the total liberation of Palestine from Israel and the creation of an Islamic state as keystones in the plan for global Islamic domination.

- Instigating a constant campaign to incite hatred by Muslims against Jews and rejecting any discussions of conciliation or coexistence with them.[43]

It looks like the Muslim Brotherhood's plan is on track as Islam and Sharia law will be the order of the day in all the Arab Spring countries. What has happened and is happening is that bad dictatorships are being replaced by far worse ones. It seems obvious to me that an Ayatollah Khomeini is far worse than Saddam Hussein and Hosni Mubarak or Bashar Assad, the current President of Syria determined to hold on to power but about to topple. What we're in for – unless the West wakes up - is Iran and Saudi Arabia multiplied by ten or twenty and, who knows, maybe a new Caliph or emperor of a worldwide Islamic empire – again! Don't forget that an Islamic empire followed the Roman Empire and ruled most of the then-known world for hundreds of years, approximately from the eighth to the nineteenth century.

We are in one of those times again when the book of Revelation is being quoted and referenced and the topic of the Antichrist frequently raised. But one of these times the would-be Bible prophets are going to be right – and it will be the last of the last days. Could it be that this is it?

BIBLE PROPHECY

A new dimension in the study of Bible prophecy, it appears to me, is the increase in the number of scholars who are former Muslims, and former Muslim terrorists and imams

---

[43] *Ibid.*, pp. 75-76.

(e.g., Reza F. Safa, Walid Shoebat, Mark A. Gabriel and others).[44] They speak with one voice about the immediate threat Islam is to all other religions and to the world-at-large. And while that may be true, according to Joel Rosenberg, in his *Inside the Revolution* (2009), Muslims are converting to Christianity in unprecedented numbers. He quotes from a live interview on Aljazeera satellite television given by Sheikh Ahmad Al Qataani, a Saudi cleric, warning Muslims of the advance of Christian faith: "In every hour, 667 Muslims convert to Christianity...Every day, 16,000 Muslims convert to Christianity. Every year, 6 million Muslims convert to Christianity." [45]

Since Rosenberg's research is among the most recent, it is important to notice his comment on the above quotation: "I cannot confirm these precise numbers. I can, however, confirm the trend lines. During the course of interviewing more than 150 Christian leaders...over the past several years, I have been able to assemble enough data and anecdotal evidence to paint a picture – albeit an imperfect and incomplete one – that provides a sense of how powerfully the God of the Bible is moving to draw Muslims into His family....there is now no question that so many people are becoming Christians in the region that Muslim leaders are becoming nervous and angry." He goes on to suggest that one significant cause for this might

---

[44] See J. Rosenberg, *Inside the Revolution: How the Followers of Jihad, Jefferson & Jesus Are Battling to Dominate the Middle East and transform the World* (Carol Stream, Illinois: Tyndale House, 2009), pp.363-368, for conversion of Tass Saada, former PLO terrorist and sniper.

[45] Ibid., p.381

have been the exposing of the true face of Islam by Ayatollah Khomeini's ferocious 1979 revolution in Iran.[46]

Rosenberg's comment, however, that this upsurge in Christian conversions has caused the Muslim leadership to be "nervous and angry" is intriguing. Could it be that there is more to the Arab Spring than gaining democratic rights and that, perhaps, more to do with throttling enthusiasm for Christian faith and entrenching Sharia law? Rosenberg is convinced that millions of Arabs have believed in Christ, but are too fearful for their lives to make it public and that the anti-Christian bias of the media maintains the silence. He discusses "The Christian Surge" in Iran, North Africa (Egypt, Libya, Algeria, Morocco), Sudan, Iraq, Israel, Syria, Lebanon, Jordan, Saudi Arabia, Afghanistan, Central Asia (Uzbekistan, Kazakhstan) and Pakistan.[47]

THE RISE OF TURKEY

Another fascinating development in the area of Bible prophecy, it seems to me, is the significance given to the rise of Turkey, especially in the teaching of Walid Shoebat. This former Muslim and Islamic terrorist, and widely travelled popular speaker and best-selling author, forcefully and eloquently argues that with the current rise of Turkey on the international scene we are seeing the pieces falling into place of a resurrected Islamic Empire. After all, Turkey was the headquarters of the Islamic Byzantine and Ottoman Empires for

---

[46] Ibid., p. 382.

[47] Ibid., pp. 381-405.

almost fourteen hundred years, ending in 1924. In Shoebat's teaching, it is not a restored Roman Empire that the Bible predicts but a resurrected Islamic Empire with, once again, Turkey as the dominant influence in the Middle East. Furthermore, it is to the Middle East - not Europe – that we need to look for the appearance of Antichrist and to Islam for his hordes of followers (Revelation 13.3-4).[48]

I must say that having been born and educated in Northern Ireland, and steeped in Protestant anti-Catholicism, it's intriguing to have somebody other than the Pope identified as the Antichrist. Not that it ever made a lot of sense to me. It was a belief I rejected in late adolescence when I was mature enough to examine it. But what Shoebat and other Bible scholars are now pointing to in the prophetic Scriptures about Turkey and Islam has the ring of accuracy about it. I find myself reading Scipture passages that puzzled me, with little or no help from various commentaries, suddenly exclaiming: "Hey, that makes sense! I can see it already happening." Almost every week the news media provide ample evidence for the rise of Turkey in Middle East politics as a mediator of first resort and of the worldwide reach of Islam as it gets the West to fight its battles for it Witness the United Nations and NATO participating in the destruction of secular Muslim administrations, albeit dictatorships, in Iran, Iraq, Tunisia, Egypt, Libya, and currently Syria, that will almost surely result in the entrenchment of Islamic Sharia law.

In his book, *God's War on Terror: Islam, Prophecy and the Bible,* Walid Shoebat quotes an article written in 2007 by

---

[48] Walid Shoebat, *God's War on Terror: Islam, Prophecy and the Bible* (United States: Top Executive Media, 2010),pp. 56, 57-182, 445-453.

What in Heaven's Name is Happening on Earth?

Professor Ruben Safrastyan, Ph.D., Director of the Department of Turkish Studies at the Institute of Oriental Studies, Armenian National Academy of Sciences : "The Government of the pro-Islamist Justice and Development Party (JDP) that came to power in 2002 restructured...the basic directions of the Turkish foreign policy...The Foreign Ministry of the country was instructed to improve relations with the Arab states and Iran, at the same time conserving allied relations with Israel on quite a cool level. *As a result Turkey will have the opportunity to get a mediating role both in the Middle East conflict and in controversial relations between some Middle-Eastern countries and the West. Therefore, Turkey will become a key state in the region,* which will enhance its significance for the European Union and accelerate the process of Turkey accession to that organization." Shoebat goes on to document Turkey's tilt towards a far more Islamist government and the increasing movement calling for restoration of the Islamist Empire. [49]

This is all the more remarkable when we remember that it was only a decade or so ago that Turkey was being hailed as a model secular Muslim nation. Professor Efraim Inbar of Bar-Ilan University, Tel Aviv, comments on Turkey's current status on the international scene: "Turkey is no longer an ally of Israel or the West. 'It is a Trojan Horse in NATO,' he says, adding that conflct with Israel serves Erdogan's [Prime Minister of Turkey] quest for hegemony in the Arab and Muslim world."

Erdogan is at the centre of this revolution in Israeli-Turkey relations. His party, the Justice and Development Party, is a conservative one with Islamist roots. In the past Turkey had good relations with Israel and bad relations with all the rest of

---

[49] *Ibid.*, pp. 431, 440-453; see also Robert Spencer, pp.170-172.

her neighbours. Now it is the opposite: Turkey is improving relationships with everyone else in the region at the expense of Israel. As one Israeli worriedly and fearfully expressed it: "We do not need to add Turkey as an enemy. We have enough enemies surrounding us, especially now with this Arab Spring, or Arab Winter, whatever you want to call it...alluding to Israel's fear that hostile Islamists will eventually replace ousted dictators in places like Egypt and Libya."[50]

ISLAM IS NOT JUST ANOTHER RELIGION

The dragon, we are told in Revelation 12:17, "was enraged at the woman [Israel] and went off to make war against the rest of her offspring – those who obey God's commandments and hold to the testimony of Jesus." Of all the great religions, historically speaking, Islam dominated Jews and Christians more than any other, not only because it lasted hundreds of years but because it never ever gave equal recognition to them. It is likely that Islam has slain more Christians by far and demolished more Churches than any other religion. [51]

Someone is sure to say "But haven't Christians killed just as many Muslims and been just as violent? The answer is "No!" The Christian Church has never endorsed the taking of human life and though exceptions have been made regarding

---

[50] M. Petrou, "Israel Alone," MACLEAN'S (Oct. 3, 2011).

[51] Shoebat, p.437; Spencer, p.99.

Capital Punishment or waging a Just War neither has been accepted universally by the Church. In fact it wasn't until the fourth century that it was acceptable for a Christian to join the army. It is true to say that from the beginning until now, the Christian Church has never been at ease or at peace with the taking of human life for any reason. Islam, to the contrary, has always endorsed war.

Jacques Ellul, renowned French theologian and philosopher, writes about "the importance and glorification of war as a means of spreading the faith" in Islam. "Such war is a duty for all Muslims. Islam has to become universal. The true faith...has to be taken to every people by every means, including by military force. This makes the political power important, for it is warlike by nature. The two things are closely related. The political head wages war on behalf of the faith. He is thus the religious head, and as the sole representative of God he must fight to extend Islam. This enormous importance of war has been totally obliterated today in intellectual circles that admire Islam and want to take it afresh as a model. War is inherent in Islam. It is inscribed in its teaching. It is a fact of its civilization and also a religious fact; the two cannot be separated. It is coherent with its conception of Dhar al ahrb, that the whole world is destined to become Muslim by Arab conquests." [52]

Ellul goes on to point out that the proof of "all this is not just theological; it is historical: hardly has the Islamic faith been preached when an immediate military conquest begins.

---

[52] J. Ellul, *The Subversion of Christianity* (Grand Rapids, Michigan: Wm. B. Erdmans, 1986), p. 100.

From 632 to 651, in the twenty years after the death of the prophet, we have a lightning war of conquest with the invasion of Egypt and Cyrenaica to the west, Arabia in the centre, Armenia, Syria and Persia to the east. In the following century all North Africa and Spain are taken over, along with India and Turkey to the east. The conquests are not achieved by sanctity, but by war." [53]

In contrast to all that, for three hundred years Christianity was spread by proclaiming God's love and demonstrating it in word and deed, by kindness, love for the poor, personal example and morality. When Constantine embraced Christianity, observes Ellul, "war was hardly tolerated by the Christians. Even when waged by a Christian emperor it was a dubious business and was assessed unfavorably. It was often condemned....In practice Christians would remain critical of war until the flamboyant image of the holy war came on the scene. In other words, no matter what atrocities have been committed in wars waged by so-called Christian nations, war has always been in essential contradiction to the gospel. Christians have always been more or less aware of this. They have judged war and questioned it....In Islam, on the contrary, war was always just and constituted a sacred duty." He states in summary: "I believe that in every respect the spirit of Islam is contrary to that of the revelation of God in Jesus Christ." [54]

What in Heaven's Name *is* Happening on Earth? God is warning us that a dark and dreadful shadow is falling across our world in the form of radical Islamist governments. The call

---

[53] *Ibid.*, pp.100-101.

[54] *Ibid.*, p.98.n

to us is for vigilance, and especially at this time when both Republican and Democratic administrations in the United States, and conservative and liberal ones in Canada, are proclaiming Islam as a civilized religion of peace and goodwill. Support for Islamic governments and political parties always seems to be forthcoming just so long as there is commitment to democracy. It doesn't seem to matter that so far the governments elected are all committed to implementing Sharia law. Did you know that the new, post-Taliban, Afghanistan constitution stipulates that "no law can be contrary to the beliefs and provisions of the sacred religion of Islam"? This constitution came into being during the watch of President George Bush.[55]

There is also Iraq, another country that has cost the West billions of dollars and thousands of lives. Since the fall and death of Saddam Hussein, half the nation's prewar 700,000 Christian population has fled including many Christian business owners. One merchant who left said that "before the war there was no separation between Christian and Muslim. Under Saddam no one asked your religion, and we used to attend each other's religious services and weddings. After the invasion we hoped democracy would come; but instead all that came was bombs, kidnapping, and killing. Now at least 75 % of my Christian friends have fled. There is no future for us in Iraq." Overall the Christian population in the Middle East has dropped from 20% in 1900 to less than 2% today."[56]

---

[55] R. Spencer, p. 48.

[56] *Ibid.*, p. 49.

Finding a Firm Foundation in a Rapidly Changing World

A recent article in MACLEAN'S magazine (June 25, 2012) asked the right question: "The Arab Spring for this?" ran the headline. The focus of the article was on the choice faced by the Egyptian people in the election of June 16-17, 2012: "A return to the Mubarak era – or sharia law? That's the choice facing voters in Egypt's presidential runoff." It was a choice between "the Muslim Brotherhood and a military backed autocracy," respectively the candidates being Mohammed Morsi and Ahmed Shafik. To one citizen it was like asking her to choose between "the plague and cholera." Morsi had the support of "Egypt's oldest and most well-organized opposition group, the Mulsim Brotherhood." Shafik had the support of the old government, the army, the security forces and the business community. Significantly, Shafik proclaimed that he would save Egypt "from the 'dark forces' of political Islam." The result of the election? The Muslim Brotherhood won – even though by a small margin.

Similar developments have happened in Libya. One political dissident, imprisoned under Gadhafi, declared that Libya "is now being controlled by a 'shadowy cabal of former Gadhafi officials, Islamists and Muslim Brothers,' in the governing National Transitional Council (NTC). This force appears likely to maintain power in Tripoli after elections for a 200-member congress charged with overseeing the drafting of a constitution….Libya's Muslim Brotherhood has emerged as the country's most organized political force, and a strong performance will mean that a third Arab Spring country could soon be controlled by Islamists, following Tunisia and Egypt. If that happens, warned another dissident, expect "a repeat of what is happening in Tunisia with pressure on women to cover up, and raids on art galleries." Another worries about the power of the Muslim Brotherhood: "They want to control this whole area, Tunisia, Egypt, Jordan, Libya, and they are gaining power every day."[57]

As I write (Aug. 2012), the same story is being told about developments in Syria. The Shia-backed government of dictator Bashar Assad is on the brink of collapsing as a fiercely fought civil war wages on. The Sunni-backed rebel army continues to gain ground every day as high level members of the government defect. What makes this different than the other Arab Spring conflicts is that Iran supports Bashar Assad, and Saudi Arabia and Qatar are behind the rebels. The latter two countries are unrelenting Islamist states. In fact fifteen of the seventeen terrorists involved in nine/eleven were from Saudi Arabia. So although the United States and Canada have already contributed millions and millions of dollars and recently committed millions more as they support the rebel army in Syria, the West loses and Islam wins no matter who wins this civil war: Syria is backed by radical Islamist Iran and the rebel leadership is heavily influenced by the Muslim Brotherhood, to say the least.

We are being told on every hand that the civil war in Syria is being waged for democracy and, of course, it is. But surely the question must be faced: What kind of democracy can be had under sharia law? When we look at those societies that live under sharia law now - Iran, Saudi Arabia, Sudan, Tunisia, Afghanistan under the Taliban, Iraq – none are democracies. Iranian journalist Amir Taheri argues that Islam is incompatible with democracy. "There are fifty-seven nations in the

---

[57] J. Dettmer, "The Forecast in Libya: Winter Ahead? In elections this week, Islamists and friends of Gadhafi jostle for power;" R. Sherlock, "'Power is in our hands'", MACLEAN'S (July 16, 2012; Sept. 12, 2011).

Organisation of the Islamic Conference (OIC). Not one is a democracy. The more Islamic the regime in place the less democratic it is."[58] Western leaders, being led by the left-leaning news media, seem oblivious to this and continue to support or to stand by while less Islamic regimes are replaced by ones more aggressively, and perhaps more radically, Islamic. It has the hallmarks of a great demonic deception: powerful western nations with hundreds of years of Christian heritage and values behind them enabling Islam with its sharia law and oppressive political program to take over nation after nation. This is what the United States, Canada and the other NATO nations have done and are doing right at this time.

What in Heaven's Name *IS* Happening on Earth? The words of the Biblical prophets are being confirmed. Every day the news media report on the Middle East using over and over again names of countries that seem more properly to belong to the Bible. These days they are being tossed about every day. How many times this year have we read reports about Egypt, Tunisia, Libya, Lebanon, Sudan, Turkey, Saudi Arabia, Iraq, Iran, Israel and now Syria more than ever (Ezekiel 35-36, 38-39; Isaiah 15-21; Zephaniah 1-3). These are all names of countries that the prophets spoke of in the context of "the last days" or "the day of the Lord."

Although the Lord Jesus told us that no one knows the day or the hour of His coming, He did tell us to be alert and watchful for the signs of His Coming: "Watch out that you are not deceived...When you hear of wars and revolutions, do not be frightened. These things must happen first, but the end will not come right away....Nation will rise against nation, and

---

[58] R. Spencer, p.166.

kingdom against kingdom....they will lay hands on you and persecute you....When you see Jerusalem surrounded by armies, you will know that desolation is near....There will be signs in the sun, moon and stars. On the earth, nations will be in anguish and perplexity at the roaring and tossing of the sea. Men will faint from terror, apprehensive of what is coming on the world....At that time they will see the Son of Man coming in a cloud with power and great glory. **When these things begin to take place, stand up and lift up your heads, because your redemption is drawing near"** (Luke 21:8-28, emphasis added).

     Wars and revolutions, arrest and persecution, natural and national disasters, leaders in anguish and perplexity – all of these we've experienced or read about over and over again. Nevertheless, the Lord Jesus told us to watch for these when they were happening on an unprecedented scale and when Jerusalem was surrounded by armies because then they would be signs of His Return. Notice that the Lord Jesus said "when these things begin to take place." What is happening in the Middle East has not happened before; that is, Muslim nations being conquered for "democracy" by Islamic armies backed by western Christian nations. How democratic they will be remains to be seen. But what is clear and obvious from what has happened in Egypt, Tunisia, Libya, Iraq and Afghanistan (and is about to happen in Syria), it is more than likely that sharia law will be entrenched in each of their constitutions. Israel, at that point, will be surrounded by nations led not by quasi-friendly Muslim dictators like Mubarak and al Assad but by Iran-like ayatollahs and imams. As one observer of the political developments in the Middle East stated: "'Now it is not the leaders who are making decisions in the Arab world. It's the people'....Among them are liberals and democrats, but also Islamists, radicals and populists, who will all wield power as

Finding a Firm Foundation in a Rapidly Changing World

their leaders wield less. 'Israel...which is used to having peace with leaders and not peace with people, is facing a new regional reality.'"[59]

SUGGESTED ORDER FOR SMALL GROUPS

PRAYER TIME

Prayers of confession, petition & intercession

BIBLE WARM-UP: The Old Testament Names of God

Jehovah-nissi (je-ho-vah-nis-ee): God our Banner or Ensign or Standard.

MEMORY VERSE

Joshua 1:8 *"Do not let this Book of the Law depart from your mouth; meditate on it day and night, so that you may be careful to do everything written in it. Then you will be prosperous and successful."*

---

[59] M. Petrou, "Israel Alone," MACLEAN'S, Oct. 3, 2011.

DAILY BIBLE READINGS: WORDS & THOUGHTS FOR FURTHER REFLECTION

Day 1: Isaiah 36

_____
_____

Day 2: Isaiah 37:1-20

_____
_____

Day 3: Isaiah 37:21-38

_____
_____

Day 4: Isaiah 38

_____
_____

Day 5: Isaiah 39

_____
_____

Finding a Firm Foundation in a Rapidly Changing World

Day 6: Isaiah 40:1-11

_____

_____

Day 7: Isaiah 40:12-31

_____

_____

DISCUSSION QUESTIONS

1. Do you agree with Michael Coren, the newspaper columnist, that the news media has an anti-Israel and a pro-Arab bias? Discuss.

2. Would you agree that this conflict between Israel and the Palestinians seems to be all about "the land," about who owns it and how it should be divided up? Discuss.

What in Heaven's Name is Happening on Earth?

3.Jihad means waging holy war against Islam's infidel enemies. What are the three stages of Jihad mentioned by the former Islamic scholar, Mark Gabriel?

4.What is the Arab Spring?

5.Read Jeremiah 31:35-36. What does this tell us about Yahweh (or Jehovah) and His relationship with Israel?

6.Based on his research, what are Joel Rosenberg's conclusions regarding Muslim conversions? Suggest some topics we can lovingly and sensitively introduce and discuss with Jews and Muslims in sharing our Christian faith with them.

7. According to Jacques Ellul, what is the difference between the Christian and the Islamic viewpoint on waging war?

CLOSING PRAYER: Heavenly Father, we come to you confessing our sins of prejudice and discrimination, pride and self-centredness. We seek humbly your forgiveness and grace and mercy. We ask, as Solomon did, for a wise and understanding heart that we might be able to love and to share your love with those we relate to from day to day. Help us to be steadfast in faith and constant in love, quick to repent and ready to forgive, and full of mercy and grace, like you, Lord Jesus. Amen and Amen.

What in Heaven's Name is Happening on Earth?

Finding a Firm Foundation in a Rapidly Changing World

CHAPTER EIGHT

ISRAEL'S MIRACULOUSLY RESTORATION AND PRESERVATION

I travel to my home in Beth El from Jerusalem on the same route that Abraham and others traveled in Bible times, from Shechem to Hebron and places in between. Today we pass many other beautiful flourishing Jewish communities along the way...When I reach the Givat Assaf intersection, I am always inspired by the large sign posted there, sponsored by our local grocer: 'Here, in Beth El, 3800 years ago, the Creator of the World promised the Land of Israel to the people of Israel. It is by virtue of this promise that we dwell today in Haifa, Tel Aviv, Shilo, and Hebron.

Rabbi Binyamin Elon[60]

Jeremiah the prophet proclaimed "This is what the LORD says, he who appoints the sun to shine by day, who decrees the moon and stars to shine by night, who stirs up the

---

[60] *God's Covenant with Israel,* quoted in D. Jeremiah, *What in the World is Going On?* (Nashville, Tenn.: Thomas Nelson, 2008), p. 6.

sea so that its waves roar – the LORD Almighty is his name: 'Only if these decrees vanish from my sight,' declares the LORD, 'will the descendants of Israel ever cease to be a nation before me" (31:35-36). For centuries that prophesy must have seemed like empty words, but at the turn of the 20th century the hand of the Lord was once more clearly evident in the destiny of the Jews.

In 1917, after Britain had taken Palestine from the Turks, the British Government announced that it favoured the establishment in Palestine of a Jewish national home. This became known as the Balfour Declaration. The League of Nations came into the picture in 1922 recognizing "the historical connection of the Jewish people with Palestine" and "the grounds for reconstituting their national home in that country" and granting Britain a mandate to administer Palestine until that object was achieved. Alas, Britain wasn't up to the job in the face of fierce Arab resistance and within the year had set the greater part of Palestine aside for an Arab state. More than three-quarters of Palestine went to establish the Arab state of Jordan in 1946. Only one quarter remained for the national homeland for the Jews.

Jewish immigrants continued to pour into Palestine. Arab attacks increased on the Jewish communities. So much so that a Jewish defence force was formed to fight back, the Haganah. This would be the nucleus of the future Israel Defence Forces. The arrival of more and more Jewish immigrants stimulated economic activities and opportunities with the result that the ranks of both Arabs and Jews swelled between the two world wars. But things got worse between Arab and Jew. One historical report stated that "matters came to a head after the Nazi mass-murder of European Jewry during

Finding a Firm Foundation in a Rapidly Changing World

World War II, when survivors attempting to enter Palestine were turned back by the British. Thwarted by the law, refugees then began to enter the country illegally, while within Palestine, Jewish underground groups embarked on anti-British acts. The situation was rapidly getting out of hand." [61]

The British had enough and gave up their mandate in April 1947, turning the whole problem over to the United Nations. By November of that year, the United Nations granted a Jewish homeland in Palestine. Only God could have done it; it had to be a miracle! The Arab nations totally rejected this and if it hadn't been for "the unexpected joint support of the U.S.A. and the U.S.S.R.", the U.N. General Assembly would not have been able to pass the motion. 33 countries voted in favour, 13 against and 10 abstaining, including Britain. Sadly, Britain lost out at this opportunity to bless Israel. The last British soldier left Palestine on May 14, 1948, and the independent Jewish state of Israel was proclaimed. "Israel is a small miracle, " wrote Barbara Amiel in MACLEAN'S magazine, "It was born of the lion and the lamb lying down together when the Soviet Union and the United States came together in 1948 to lead the drive to create the state. Perhaps, God willing, a small miracle could happen again" (Jan. 11, 1988). Well, He was and is – many times over!

On the day that Israel declared its rebirth as a nation all hell broke loose. All the armies of Syria, Lebanon, Jordan, Egypt and Iraq invaded Israel in an attempt to throttle the infant

---

[61] Carta's *Historical Atlas of Israel;* F. M. Schweitzer, *A History of the Jews Since The First Century A.D.* (New York: THE MACMILLAN COMPANY., 1971), PP.285-295; *also Baker's Bible Atlas* (Grand Rapids, Michigan: Baker Book House, 1961), pp. 249-250.

nation at its birth. Nothwithstanding millions of Arabs, the tiny nation not only defeated those five armies but expanded her borders. Between February and July, 1949, Israel and its Arab neighbours signed an armistice agreement in which "Israel retained the whole of Galilee, the coastal plain, a corridor leading from the plain to Jerusalem, and all of the Negev except the Gaza district along the Mediterranean coast. That was The War of Independence – there would be another three like it![62]

Not only is it a miracle, I believe, that Israel was restored as a nation – millions of Jews scattered all over the earth returning to a little slice of land on the Mediterranean coast – but also that its restoration has endured and progressed. That in spite of huge odds against it: terrorist attack after attack, war after war in which Israel's army was outnumbered at least four to one, including more and more modern weaponry in every category: tanks, aircraft, missiles and artillery. Israel not only survived all this but increased in population and established herself as a nation. For me there is no doubt: "This is the Lord's doing and it is marvelous in our eyes"(Psalm 118:23).

IN SPITE OF OPPOSITION

Furthermore, the opposition to the rebirth of Israel didn't come only from the Arabs. Other countries refused to help because of fear of offending the Arab nations and losing their source of cheap oil. Even before the Second World War, it was known that millions of Jews would be in danger of their

---

[62] *Ibid.*

lives if they were not permitted to immigrate to Palestine. Still the British authorities in Palestine refused entry to returning Jews, and continued to block entry even though they knew of the Nazi holocaust. The limit imposed in 1939 was 2,000 per month and kept in place until the British left in 1948. Not even the knowledge of six million Jews perishing at the hands of the Nazis would change their restrictive immigration policy.

Britain wasn't the only country that was reluctant and hesitant about helping the Jews re-establish their nation. When 900 Jews fled the Nazis on the S.S. St. Louis in 1939 to seek asylum across the Atlantic, the refugees on the St. Louis tried the South American countries first. They were met with hostility and resistence. So they tried the U.S. and were driven away by navy gunboats. They tried Canada and to our shame we refused asylum and sent them back to Europe, where most of them – including children – perished in the Nazi gas chambers. Only two years ago, my wife Maidra and I participated in a Watchmen for the Nations event in Ottawa, which had brought the survivors of the St. Louis, about 30 people, to Canada in order to apologize to them and ask for their forgiveness. It was an emotional event, highly appreciated by the Jewish survivors, and a step towards national repentance for our treatment of the Jews. Significantly, I think, the Canadian Churches were well-represented, and other faiths, including the First Nations. There were no widely known government representatives there, although correspondence was read including a letter from the Leader of the Opposition, Stockwell Day.

A FLOOD OF IMMIGRANTS

What in Heaven's Name is Happening on Earth?

After 1948, when Israel was reborn as a nation, the floodgates of immigration opened to the remnant of Jews left in the world, after the horrendous loss of six million. Within three years, almost 700,000 immigrated, more than half of them from Europe. For Israel, that meant a doubling of the population. It also meant that nearly half of all surviving Jews in Central and Eastern Europe (excluding the Soviet Union) had moved to Israel. One authority on the subject comments: "In some cases the percentage was much higher. Of Bulgarian Jews, for example, some 80 percent immigrated to Israel. This welcome stream was eventually stemmed by restrictions imposed by the authorities in Eastern bloc countries. Hence, Aliyah [immigration] from Western Europe became the main source of European immigration until the 1970's, when Russia once again permitted some immigration to Israel."[63]

In the Middle East, the rebirth of Israel as a nation had an electrifying effect on the Jewish communities in the Arab countries. Aided by the harsh and repressive backlash in many situations, many Jewish famiies, sometimes whole communities, left everything and came to Israel. "Operation Eagle's Wings" (I wonder if someone had read Revelation 12:14!) referred to the moving by air of 45,000 Jews from Yemen in 1949. Then came "Operation Magic Carpet" in 1950-51 when about 90% of the Jewish community in Iraq, about 150,000, many arriving with only the clothes on their backs. Likewise many Jews arrived from Egypt, Libya, Tunisia, Algeria and Morocco.

UNRELENTING HOSTILITY

---

[63] *Carta's Historical Atlas of Israel.*

Finding a Firm Foundation in a Rapidly Changing World

Although Egypt, Jordan, Lebanon and Syria signed the Armistice after the War of Independence in 1949, they still considered themselves in a state of war with Israel. Armed infiltrators on suicide missions, called *Fidayun*, came from Egypt and Jordan murdering and sabotaging and disrupting the Israeli settlements. The Arab states carried on the war on the economic front by organizing a trade boycott and by Egypt blockading the Strait of Tiran, thereby cutting off trade with Africa and Southeast Asia." [64]

In October 1956, the Egyptian President, Gamal Abdul Nasser, made his intentions clear: newly armed with Soviet weaponry, he gathered an army in Sinai to attack Israel. But Israel, not about to sit and wait to be attacked, struck first and routed the Egyptian army in days. Israel occupied the entire Sinai peninsula and lifted the blockade in the Strait of Tiran. Now it just happened that France and Britain were furious at Nasser during this time as he had seized the Suez Canal in July, 1956, and began shelling his military installations. Egypt was saved only by the intervention of the United States and the Soviet Union acting together in compelling a withdrawal from the Sinai and the stationing of United Nations troops along the old border between Egypt and Israel. Why this intervention by the U.S. and U.S.S.R.? Probably because they feared the likelihood of Middle East oil falling into the hands of France and Britain. "O, what tangled webs we weave....!"

THE SIX-DAY WAR

---

[64] *Ibid.*

What in Heaven's Name is Happening on Earth?

Nasser bounced back again after the war in 1956: again, abundantly supplied by the Soviet Union, he gathered an army in Sinai making no bones about his intention to destroy Israel. Allied with Syria and Jordan, Nasser dismissed the United Nations troops and re-instituted the blockade of the Strait of Tiran. War broke out on June 5, 1967.

But it was a short one! Only six days! Early in the war, Israel launched a lightning air strike, in which multiple flights of fighter bombers were coordinated so that they would arrive on target simultaneously in Egypt. It was a brilliantly planned and executed stroke and within about 30 minutes the entire Egyptian Airforce was demolished. "Every airfield was hit at approximately the same time" observed Hal Lindsey in his book *The Everlasting Hatred: The Roots of Jihad*, "Reconnaissance photos showed at each airfield in Egypt, almost every warplane had been hit dead center. In six days, the outnumbered Israeli Defense Forces destroyed the combined armies of the Muslim Middle East" (p. 213).

Another author summarized the rest of The Six Day War in these words: "In the swift campaigns which followed, Israel won, in six days, the whole of Judea and Samaria (the area also known as the West Bank), the Golan Heights, the Gaza district and the Sinai peninsula. A stirring event in the war was the taking of eastern Jerusalem – the Western ('Wailing') Wall and the site of the Temple – passed into Jewish hands and, for the first time in nearly two thousand years, became accessible for free and unhampered worship. Also for the first time, Israeli Moslems were able to visit and pray at their holy places – the Al-Aqsa Mosque and the Dome of the Rock." [65]

---

[65] *Ibid.*

Finding a Firm Foundation in a Rapidly Changing World

THE YOM KIPPUR WAR

A little over six years later they were at it again. Hatred and hostility had just been simmering and bubbling since the Six-Day War. This time Egypt and Syria were better able to use the new Soviet weaponry against Israel. A new Soviet anti-tank missile and a SAM missile for intercepting low-flying aircraft wreaked havoc with the Israeli artillery and airforce. An Israeli tank commander recalled that they were down to just three tanks on the Golan Heights and knew they were all that was standing between the Syrian army and Galilee. "When the Syrian commander could see only three tanks blocking his way," he related, "he said, 'It's too easy – this must be a trap.' So he ordered his forces to stop while they analyzed the situation. He reasoned the Israelis were, after all, already beaten." It gave the Israeli's enough time to rush reinforcements to the front and drive the Syrian army back. By "a miracle of God" the invaders had been sidetracked and went no further into Israel. The tank commander attributed their success "to God's protective care over Israel."

The war was launched by Egypt and Syria simultaneously on October 6, 1973, Israel's holiest day of the year, Yom Kippur, the Day of Atonement. Only a bare minimum of soldiers were on duty. Unlike past conflicts, Israel sustained heavy losses in personnel and equipment. Casualties were the highest yet as the Arabs won more battles than ever before: "Hardened and confident combat units were so outnumbered and outflanked they were fleeing in disarray. Israel lost more than 500 tanks and 49 aircraft in the first three days alone." The situation looked so hopeless at times that, according to Hal

Lindsey, the Defense Minister Moshe Dayan recommended to Prime Minister Golda Meier the "Sampson Option," the use of nuclear weapons. "The Sampson Option," writes Lindsey, "is a fully operational plan to be used if Muslim forces overrun Israel. If the plan is implemented, every Arab capitol will be vaporized in a thermonuclear mushroom cloud. Only now the warheads will be delivered by Jericho II missiles instead of aircraft."[66]

The war came to an end on October 22, 1973, after the United Nations intervened in voting a cease-fire.

DEALS WITH DIPLOMATS AND TERRORISTS!

Since the end of the Yom Kippur War Israel has been engaged in diplomatic agreements with Egypt in 1973-4; with Syria, 1974; again with Egypt in 1977 resulting in the historic Egypt-Israel Peace Treaty signed by Anwar Sadat and Menachem Begin (in which Israel gave up the Sinai Peninsula, military and naval bases, airfields, and oilfields for the normalization of relations with Egypt); with Lebanon in 1982; and then the Madrid Conference in 1991 with Yasser Arafat representing the Palestinians. Since that time it has been an ongoing conflict between Israel and the Palestinians, with Yasser Arafat being the unquestioned spokesperson and leader until his death in 2006. The cost in lives and property has been horrendous as the Palestinians took to the streets and increasingly used suicide bomb martyrs.

---

[66] H. Lindsey, *The Everlasting Hatred: The Roots of Jihad* (Oracle House Publishing, Murrieta 92562, p. 215.

Finding a Firm Foundation in a Rapidly Changing World

Two more far-reaching diplomatic agreements during this time need to be considered separately and to bring us up to the present time: the Oslo Peace Accords of 1993 and the U.S. sponsored Roadmap to Peace of 2003. They set the stage for our discussion of future things, including what's in store for Israel and the Church of Christ worldwide. Does Israel still have a place in God's Plan? Or was Israel's place taken over by the Church? We'll grapple with those questions in our next chapter.

SUGGESTED ORDER FOR SMALL GROUPS

APPROACHING WITH PRAISE AND WORSHIP

Choruses of prayers of praise, thanksgiving and adoration

PRAYER TIME

Prayers of confession, petition & intercession

BIBLE WARM-UP: The Old Testament Names of God

Jehovah-M'Kaddesh (je-ho-vah-m-kad-desh): God our Sanctifier.

MEMORY VERSE

What in Heaven's Name is Happening on Earth?

John 1:29 *"The next day John saw Jesus coming toward him and said, "Look, the Lamb of God, who takes away the sin of the world!"*

DAILY BIBLE READINGS: WORDS & THOUGHTS FOR FURTHER REFLECTION

Day 1: Isaiah 41:1-16

_____
_____

Day 2: Isaiah 41:17-29

_____
_____

Day 3: Isaiah 42:1-9

_____
_____

Day 4: Isaiah 42:10-25

_____
_____

Finding a Firm Foundation in a Rapidly Changing World

Day 5: Isaiah 43:1-13

_____

_____

Day 6: Isaiah 43:14-28

_____

_____

Day 7: Isaiah 44:1-11

_____

_____

DISCUSSION QUESTIONS

1. Review last week's topic. Would you agree that Psalm 118:23 is an apt description of Israel's rebirth as a nation? Discuss.

2. Canada hasn't been a great supporter of Israel under any of the Liberal governments since before the Second World War (e.g., the S.S. St. Louis refugees in 1939 being turned away). Given what God said in Genesis 12:3, should this be a matter of concern for all political parties?

3. Read Jeremiah 16:14-15. Before 1948 the talk was all about Israel's exodus from Egypt under Moses. According to this scripture, what is the new exodus that was prophesied?

4. Read about the valley of dry bones in Ezekiel 37. It's about Israel's rebirth. How long does it say that Israel will dwell in the land after they come back? (see vs. 11-12, 21, 25)

5. The Psalmist over and over again talks about the Lord being Israel's "refuge" and "high tower" and her "fortress." How do we engage lovingly and sensitively our Jewish friends in discussing the essential requirement of Salvation to embrace and love the Lord Jesus?

6. What about the Six Day War? Can you see Divine intervention at work?

7. What about the Yom Kippur War? What was the "Sampson Option" that was considered being used by the Israeli Defense Minister?

CLOSING PRAYER: What a great and mighty God you are, our Father! You save and deliver your people, you protect and preserve them. How wonderfully faithful you are to your promises; you never fail us nor forsake us. You are the God who is there – always! Thank you for watching over us as a tender, loving Shepherd looks after his sheep. You are such a good God, faithful and true. Help us to be like you, Father! In Jesus' Name, we pray. Amen.

What in Heaven's Name is Happening on Earth?

Finding a Firm Foundation in a Rapidly Changing World

PART THREE: WHAT IN HEAVEN'S NAME *WILL* HAPPEN ON EARTH?

What in Heaven's Name is Happening on Earth?

CHAPTER NINE

GOD WILL KEEP HIS COVENANT WITH ISRAEL!

Let us take courage, and in the name of God let us set up our banners. He who has been with us up to now will preserve us to the end, and we will soon sing in the fruition of glory as we now recite in the confidence of faith: that His purpose is completed and His love immutable.

Charles Spurgeon[67]

THE PROPAGANDA WAR

The western media have pulled off something that is so deceptive and clever that it is hard to fathom. They have convinced the world that big bad Israel has cheated and abused, robbed and humiliated the poor, downtrodden and helpless Arabs. In spite of the fact that Israel's population is only five million, its land about half the size of the province of Alberta,

---

[67] *THE ESSENTIAL WORKS OF CHARLES SPURGEON* (Uhrichsville, Ohio: Barbour Publishing, 2009), p. 912.

What in Heaven's Name is Happening on Earth?

while there are two-hundred and forty million Arabs in the Middle East, many of them fabulously rich in oil money, and over a billion Muslims worldwide. Who hasn't heard the propaganda slogans: "Land for Peace," "The legitimate rights of the Palestinians," "Israeli aggression in the occupied territories," "End the 'Occupation' of Palestinian land." That the world media has bought into this, I think, is largely because of concessions made by Israel in the Oslo Peace Accords in 1993. To state this, of course, is not to condone abusing the poor, racial exploitation, or economic oppression in any form whether in Israel or any other nation.

THE OSLO PEACE ACCORDS OF 1993

Meeting in secret for eighteen months at various places in Norway, representatives of the Palestinians and Israel came up with an agreement mediated by Norwegian Foreign Minister Johan Jorgen Holst. The key representative for Israel was Foreign Minister Shimon Peres. In return for recognition of Israel's right to exist as a nation, and for a promise of peaceful coexistence, Israel granted Palestinian self-rule in the Gaza Strip and the West Bank and agreed to withdraw all troops from these territories by April 13, 1994. It was signed on September 13, 1993, at the White House, and witnessed by 3,000 guests. Hosted by President Clinton, the ceremony included the shaking of hands by Israeli Prime Minister Yitzhak Rabin and Palestine Liberation Organization Chairman Yasser Arafat after they had signed the Declaration of Principles. The focal point of the peace accord was Israel's transfer to the Palestinians of all "powers and responsibilities" in the Gaza Strip and the city of Jericho. The declaration said that the Palestinians would rule themselves until December 1998, at which time a permanent agreement would be signed. They would police themselves with PLO soldiers who had been trained in Jordan. The issue of Jerusalem was such a prickly one that it was set aside to be negotiated in 1998.

True to form, shortly after the signing Yasser Arafat declared that the *intifadah,* or Palestinian uprising, would not end until Israel withdrew from what he considered "all" the Palestinian territories, including East Jerusalem. The Accord accomplished nothing for Israel, it seems, but was a huge boost to the Palestinian cause. It is probably true to say that more people have died or been injured since the peace accord was signed than before, with the great increase in suicide bombings and Israeli military responses.

THE ULTIMATE GOAL

Indeed, it seems the Oslo Accords weren't intended to bring peace, at least from the Palestinian point of view. Faisal Husseini, Arafat's Jerusalem representative, and widely believed to be the most moderate of the Palestinian leadership, revealed on May 31, 2001, what the underlying purpose was to an Egyptian newspaper: "We must distinguish the strategies and long-term goals from the political phased goals which we are compelled to accept due to international pressures." But the "ultimate goal is the liberation of all of historical Palestine." He said bluntly: "Oslo has to be viewed as a Trojan Horse." He went on to speak even more candidly of Palestinian deception saying that it is the obligation of all Palestinian forces and factions to see the Oslo Accords as temporary steps and gradual goals, because in this way "we are setting an ambush for the Israelis and cheating them."[68]

This was nothing new; it had been said even more clearly before. Is it intentional blindness or wishful thinking that hinders Israel and the nations that pressure her into treaties and agreements from seeing that Islam will stop at nothing less than the destruction of Israel?[69] Another Palestinian executive committee member, Zahir Muhsein, stated the following in an interview with a Dutch newspaper in 1977: "The Palestinian people does not exist. The creation of a Palestinian state is only a means for continuing our struggle against the state of Israel for our Arab unity. In reality, today, there is no difference between Jordanians, Palestinians, Syrians, and Lebanese. Only for political and tactical reasons do we speak today about the existence of a Palestinian people, since Arab national interests demand that we posit the existence of distinct 'Palestinian people' to oppose Zionism….For tactical reasons, Jordan, which is a sovereign state with defined borders, cannot raise claims to Haifa and Jaffa, while as a Palestinian, I can undoubtedly demand Haifa, Jaffa, Beer-Sheva and Jerusalem. However, the moment we reclaim our right to all of Palestine, we will not wait even a minute to unite Palestine and Jordan."[70]

So far the Palestinians have adhered to their stated intentions and political strategies. Israel began fulfilling the commitments made in the Oslo Accords. Accepting the idea of

---

[68] *Dispatch from Jerusalem* (Jerusalem: Bridges for Peace Publications), July-Aug., 2002, p. 16.

[69] See Revelation 20:3.

[70] Quoted in *Dispatch from Jerusalem*, July-Aug., 2002, p. 17.

"another" Palestinian state, alongside Jordan with its 70% Palestinian population and Arab King, "Israel brought in Yasser Arafat and 50,000 of his Tanzim fighters from Tunisia," wrote Clarence H. Wagner Jr. in *Dispatch from Jerusalem*, a Christian pro-Jewish magazine, "Israel armed them in hopes they would be a 'peace force' to work alongside the Israel Defense Force(IDF) for civil peace. Israel gave territory to the Palestinian Authority (PA), placing 98% of the Palestinian population of Judea and Samaria (the West Bank) and Gaza under full Palestinian authority. Israel turned over government portfolios to the PA as they stepped towards a future Palestinian state. Israel sent diplomats around the world to raise money for the fledgling PA to help develop infrastructure necessary for a new state to exist." Israel – under tremendous pressure by the U.S. - did all of this on the word of Arafat and the other Palestinian and Arab leaders that they really wanted peacefully to coexist – even though these same people had rarely kept any of their previous treaties and agreements.

On September 13, 1993, the day on which Yitzak Rabin and Yasser Arafat signed the Declaration of Principles and shook hands before all television cameras on the White House lawn, within hours Arafat was on Jordanian TV telling the truth behind the signing: "Since we cannot defeat Israel in war, we do this in stages. We take any and every territory that we can of Palestine, and establish a sovereignty there, and we use it as a springboard to take more. When the time comes, we can get the Arab nations to join us for the final blow against Israel."[71]

---

[71] *Ibid.*

What in Heaven's Name is Happening on Earth?

THE ROAD MAP TO PEACE

That was in 1993. Arafat was true to his word and the soldiers trained to keep peace have been enemies within the gate – in bringing in Arafat and his 50,000 fighters, Israel brought her enemies close to her bosom. Ten years later and thousands of injured and dead, there was a new "peace agreement" in the works, "Road Map to Peace - the U.S. sponsored, but endorsed by the "Quartet" of the United Nations, the European Union, Russia and the U.S. (the first time, I believe, that Russia has been included in official talks on the Middle East), representing ALL THE NATIONS OF THE WORLD.

Launched by President George Bush on June 24, 2002, this plan committed the U.S. to fully support a Palestinian homeland envisioning "two states, living side by side in peace and security". UN Secretary General Kofi Annan supported the Plan and called upon Israel and the Palestinians to embrace it and "bring an end to a long and painful conflict." It called for an immediate ceasefire, a crackdown on Palestinian terrorists, an Israeli withdrawal from Palestinian towns and the dismantling of Jewish settlements erected since 2001. It also called for new Palestinian leadership with a new Prime Minister and the ouster of Arafat. My local newspaper, *The Lethbridge Herald,* reported on May 1, 2003, that a new Prime Minister, Mahmoud Abbas, had been sworn in, officially beginning the new peace initiative and that "a Palestinian state with provisional borders could be established by year's end, with full statehood possible within three years, according to the timetable." However, the jury was still out as to whether Prime Minister Abbas was still taking his orders from Arafat and that what the world was witnessing was the old "Good cop/Bad cop" routine WRIT LARGE as the Palestinians forged on towards their goal of annihilating Israel.

Remembering the past sorry and sad history of "peace initiatives", an Israeli official warned that "it is crucial that we do not ... talk peace by day and have Israelis blown up by night." His statement was prophetic, because that is exactly what happened since April 30, 2003, when the "Road Map" was officially launched by the U.S. Over the next few months, it seemed the media never tired of reporting the "blows against", the "setbacks to", and the "end of" the "U.S. Road Map to Peace". I have not heard or read recently a credible commentator on the Middle East who thinks the Road Map has a hope in succeeding.

ALL THE NATIONS!

The most significant thing that is new, at least from a Bible prophecy viewpoint, is that the Quartet that sponsored the Road Map represents "all the nations" of the world. In predicting the end of all of this, the Bible repeatedly states that God will keep His covenant with Israel - not because Israel deserves it but because of the honour of His own Name–and that "all the nations" would become involved (see Joel 3:2; Zechariah 12:3). "You have disgraced my holy name among the nations," Ezekiel was told to tell Israel, "where you now live. So you don't deserve what I'm going to do for you. I will lead you home to bring honor to my name and to show foreign nations that I am holy...I will gather you from the foreign nations and bring you home"(Ezekiel 36: 22, 24 CEV). Furthermore, the Scriptures indicate He will simply not allow Israel to give away the Land – because it's not hers to give: it's His! In Ezekiel 36:5 the Lord says, "In my burning zeal I have spoken against the rest of the nations, and against all Edom [the collective name for

Arabs], for with glee and with malice in their hearts they made MY land their own possession so that they might plunder its pastureland" (emphasis added). Also Joel 2:18 "Then the Lord will be jealous for HIS land and take pity on HIS people" (emphasis added).

God's ownership of the land is the major point of a book published within months of 9/11. Entitled *Israel: The Blessing or The Curse,* the authors trace the whole "peace for land" negotiations (i.e., peace for Israel in return for land to be given to the Palestinians) back to the first President Bush. They also believe that God has frustrated all of these efforts and used natural catastrophies and disasters to judge those sponsoring such agreements and the Israeli leaders involved. They quote Joel 3:2-3 "I will gather all nations and bring them down to the Valley of Jehoshaphat. There I will enter into judgment against them concerning my inheritance, my people Israel, for they scattered my people among the nations and DIVIDED up my land" (emphasis added).

Israel: The Blessing or The Curse gives example after example of what it calls "warning-judgments" on the U.S. because it has pressured Israel to give up or "divide" land that belongs to God. Each time the U.S. has done this natural disasters have occurred and hundreds of lives lost and millions of dollars of property ruined: for example, monster storms as on October 30, 1991, when President Bush Sr. was at the Madrid peace conference his seafront home in Kennnebunkport, Maine, was being hammered by waves thirty feet high; or hurricanes like Hurricane Andrew smashing into southern Florida as the Madrid Conference convened in Washington, D.C., in August 1992. The book discusses at least 20 such happenings, including a list of 14 between President Clinton and Arafat entitled "The

Finding a Firm Foundation in a Rapidly Changing World

Results of Meeting with Yasser Arafat"(pp. 103-4). The latter not only deals with natural disasters of those meetings but also of the sexual scandal fallout that came upon President Clinton during this time:

- September 1, 1993: President Clinton announced he will meet Arafat and Rabin on September 13 in Washington, D.C., to begin the Oslo peace accords. After nearly a week of meandering in the Atlantic Ocean, Hurricane Emily hits North Carolina on this day.

- March 2, 1997: Arafat meets with President Clinton in Washington, D.C. The same day, awesome tornado storms unleash tremendous damage in Arkansas and flooding in Kentucky and Ohio. Arkansas and Kentucky declared disaster areas.

- January 21, 1998: President Clinton is waiting to meet with Arafat at the White House. At this exact time, the president's sex scandal breaks.

- September 27, 1998: Arafat is meeting with the president in Washington. Hurricane George hits Alabama and stalls. The hurricane stalls until Arafat leaves and then it dissipates. Parts of Alabama declared a disaster area.

- October 17, 1998: Arafat comes to the Wye Plantation meeting. Incredible rains fall on Texas, which cause record flooding. Parts of Texas are declared a disaster area.

- November 23, 1998: Arafat comes to America. He meets with President Clinton who is raising funds for the Palestinian state. On this day the stock market fell 216 points.

- December 12, 1998: On this day the U.S. House of Representatives votes to impeach President Clinton. At the very time of the impeachment, the president is meeting with Arafat in Gaza over the peace process.

- March 23, 1999: Arafat meets with Clinton in Washington, D.C. Market falls 219 points that day. The next day Clinton orders attack on Serbia.

- September 3, 1999: Secretary of State Albright meets with Arafat in Israel. Hurricane Dennis comes ashore on this very day after weeks of changing course in the Atlantic Ocean.

- September 22, 1999: Arafat meets with Clinton in Washington, D.C. The day before and after the meeting, the market falls more than 200 points each day. This was the first time in history the market lost more than 200 points for two days in a week. The market lost 524 points this week.

- June 16, 2000: Arafat meets with President Clinton. The market falls 265 points on this day.

Finding a Firm Foundation in a Rapidly Changing World

- July 12-26, 2000: Arafat at the Camp David meetings. Powerful droughts throughout the country. Forest fires explode in West into uncontrolled fires. By the end of August, 7 million acres are burnt.

- November 9, 2000: Arafat meets with President Clinton at the White House to try and salvage the peace process. This was just two days after the presidential election. The nation was just entering into an election crisis which was the worst in over one hundred years.

- November 11, 2001: Arafat speaks at the U.N. General Assembly and condemns Israel. He later meets with Secretary of State Colin Powell. On this day, Saddam Hussein threatens the U.S. with nuclear weapons. Within twenty-four hours of meeting with Powell, an airplane crashes in NYC killing two hundred sixty-five people. The crash was fifteen miles from where Arafat spoke.

The book mentions that repeatedly these parallel occurrences, i.e., meetings to discuss "peace for land" and calamities befalling the U.S., often were published side-by-side in the daily newspapers. I happened to have just read that in the book, when I picked up *The Lethbridge Herald*, our local newspaper, and sure enough, there it was on page A8, May 11, 2003: "Palestinians call on Israel to launch U.S. peace plan," an article about the arrival of U.S. Secretary of State Colin Powell to promote the "Road Map to Peace" plan, and right beside it was the headline, "Worst week ever for tornadoes". The article on the tornadoes began with "It was the most active week of tornadoes on record, as scores of twisters ripped across the U.S. midsection, reducing hundreds of homes and businesses to splinters and piles of loose bricks."

Could it be that what's happening in North America and in the world at large – some of it seeming so bizarre and so sudden – has to do with pressuring Israel to give up land for a Palestinian state? *Israel: The Blessing or The Curse* insists dogmatically that there is no doubt about that. The book states that the Bush administration was about to unveil its new policy when 9/11 happened: "On October 2, 2001, the major news sources reported that at the time of the attack on 9/11, the U.S. government was in the process of recognizing a Palestinian state. Just prior to September 11, the Bush administration had formulated a policy of recognizing a Palestinian state with East Jerusalem as its capital. The secretary of state, on September 13, was going to notify the Saudi Arabian ambassador of this plan. The plan was going to be announced by the secretary of state at the U.N. General Assembly on September 23. The attack on September 11 derailed this plan. At the very time the U.S. was going to force Israel into co-existence with terrorists that were dedicated to the destruction of the Jewish nation, the U.S. came under attack by the same terrorists!"(p.98) The plan was eventually made public as the Road Map to Peace and became the policy directing the peace process in the Middle East.

MYTHS

This diplomatic effort by President Bush, according to Hal Lindsey, author of numerous books on Bible prophecy, was disastrously flawed because it was based on obviously wrong

Finding a Firm Foundation in a Rapidly Changing World

assumptions and "myths". He lists these "myths" and "Facts" on WorldNetDaily: Time for Middle East reality, Aug. 22, 2003:

Myth: the "roadmap" was not supposed to begin implementation until a new qualified prime minister – who is not under Arafat's control – was elected by the people.

Fact: Mahmoud Abbas openly said that Arafat was ultimately in control of all negotiation decisions and that he had final authority. This should indicate to even a neophyte political student that the most basic, stated requirement for "the plan" was not there.

Myth: After Israel gave one unreciprocated concession after another, Abbas still claims after each new terrorist atrocity that he is unable to do anything about it because he doesn't have the freedom or the resources to deal with it.

Fact: Abbas has over 20,000 armed and trained militiamen under his command. Hamas only has about 1,200 members. He knows where they are and can get to them easily. But he has not even tried to arrest one of them.

Myth: Erecting a security fence and keeping Palestinians inside what they claim is "their territory" is against peace, and forces unbearable economic problems on them.

Fact: Palestinians have not built an economic infrastructure of their own and still have to work for the Israelis to survive.

Reality: The Palestinian people have been given more billions of dollars in aid than any other people in history. Arafat has used much of it to arm the territory to the teeth with assault weapons, to teach hatred toward the Israelis and to blame them for their miserable conditions.

Myth: Hamas, a Palestinian terrorist organization, remains committed to the ceasefire that was negotiated with Mahmoud Abbas.

Fact: A bus that was filled with women and children was deliberately targeted for destruction by a 29-year-old Palestinian schoolteacher who had a wife, two children of his own, and a nail studded bomb.

Reality: Responsibility for the destruction of 20 mostly women and children and the shredding of 100 more – 40 percent of them children – was claimed by Hamas.

JERUSALEM: THE UNMOVABLE ROCK

The world is in turmoil at this present time and will continue to be because God keeps His covenants and He is in the process of keeping His covenant with Israel. He is committed to her preservation as a nation. Repeatedly Israeli leaders, like Yitsak Rabin, Shimon Peres, Ehud Barak, have been willing, many believe too willing and too generous, to give up land for peace only to see the Palestinian leaders walk away from the meetings. Why? Most of the time because of the city of Jerusalem. To the great surprise of many, Prime Minister Ehud Barak was willing even to give up most of East Jerusalem – but Arafat and Islam want all of Jerusalem and will not settle for less. Jerusalem is like a jewel, it seems, that neither side will give up.

Finding a Firm Foundation in a Rapidly Changing World

There are key Scriptures that give us in general terms the prophetic timetable for the end times. One of them is in Zechariah 12:2-3 "I am going to make Jerusalem a cup that sends all the surrounding peoples reeling...On that day, when all the nations of the earth are gathered against her, I will make Jerusalem an immovable rock for all the nations. All who try to move it will injure themselves."

David Dolan, an American journalist and longtime resident of Jerusalem, points out in his insightful and well-written book, *ISRAEL IN CRISIS: WHAT LIES AHEAD?*, that Jerusalem as part of the prophetic endtime puzzle didn't fall into place until the Oslo Accords of 1993. He wrote: "Ironically, the essential piece of the prophetic puzzle has been moving into its prophesied position because of peace! It was the U.S. and Russian-sponsored Arab-Israeli 'peace process' of the 1990s that led to important prophetic movement concerning Jerusalem. In particular, it was Israel's written commitment to *negotiate the status* of her most sacred city that really set the last days' ball rolling"(p.45). Dolan goes on to state that Egyptian President Anwar Sadat had demanded that the final status of Jerusalem be on the table at Camp David in 1978 but Jimmy Carter was able to persuade him and Israeli Prime Minister Menachem Begin to postpone that to a later stage of the process. Dolan adds, "Bill Clinton didn't even try, realizing that the explosive topic could no longer be deflected." It came unto the table during the secret talks in Norway that led up to the signing of the Oslo Peace Accords.

Christians have spoken of the importance of Jerusalem in the last days ever since the Lord Jesus predicted the destruction of Jerusalem by the Romans in A.D. 70 and the scattering of the Jews throughout the world in Luke 21:24 "They will fall by the sword and will be taken as prisoners to all the nations. Jerusalem will be trampled on by the Gentiles until the times of the Gentiles are fulfilled." Hal Lindsey comments that "Jesus made this prophecy just before his death. He predicted the destruction and dispersion of the nation would fall upon the generation that rejected Him. His words came true 37 years later." He then adds: "The second half of this prophecy *puts a time limit* on the period of Jerusalem's desolations and captivity. Jesus forewarned it would be only 'UNTIL the times of the Gentiles are fulfilled. The 'times of the Gentiles' – their world domination – began a final countdown in June of 1967 with Israel's capture of old Jerusalem. The process will be completed with the coming of the Messiah to set up God's Kingdom."[72]

I have not heard or read any Middle East expert who thinks that Israel will give up Jerusalem. Israel has already shown that a shared arrangement would be acceptable but there has not been a hint that the Old City was negotiable. David Dolan believes that Israel will never give Jerusalem up because it contains Judaism's holiest sites on earth and that after separation from it for centuries would never cede sovereignty over it to the Muslims. As Israeli leaders have pointed out, it would certainly lead to civil strife on an unprecedented scale and likely assassination for the leader, as happened to Israeli Prime Minister Yitzhak Rabin, who signed the Oslo Accords in 1993.

On the other side, although it is not Islam's holiest site, the Noble Sanctuary (the Temple Mount) is the third most sacred place to Muslims (along with Mecca and Medina). Islam

---

[72] H. Lindsey, *The Everlasting Hatred: The Roots of Jihad*, p.228.

believes that Muhammad flew on a winged horse named Barak to the Temple Mount in Jerusalem, escorted by the angel Michael, and ascended to the seventh heaven from the great rock on top of the Temple Mount. After returning to the rock, he flew back to Mecca. For Islam not to have Jerusalem is to call into question the very honour and authority of the Koran. To settle for anything less than all of the Old City would place any Palestinian leader in the gravest of danger. Dolan reveals that Arafat pointed this out to Clinton and Barak at Camp David "saying it was the main reason be would have to refuse Barak's rather generous concessions on Jerusalem. He said the compromise proposals simply did not go far enough to save his skin from the wrath of Palestinian Muslim militants." [73]

A CUP OF INTOXICATION

As we read in Zechariah 12:2-3 that Jerusalem will be "a cup of intoxication" to Israel's neighbouring nations and an "immovable rock" to all the nations. Those that try to remove Jerusalem from Israel will only hurt themselves! That's exactly what Islam is trying to accomplish through Mahmoud Abbas, the Palestinian people, and the oil-rich Arab nations. They believe and are convinced that's what their duty to Allah requires. Because of their control over most of the world's oil reserves, they have the attention of the world's most powerful nations. That's why "all the nations" will gather for war "because of Jerusalem." But that's another story for another time. That's Armageddon!

---

[73] Dolan, p. 46.

What in Heaven's Name is Happening on Earth?

So on the world goes down the road following the "Road Map to Peace," pinning its hopes on the "reasonableness" of politicians and diplomats. We must be thankful that, at least, some effort is being made to attain peace in our world – think how horrendous it would be to be in a continuous state of war. And yet that is the way it has been in Israel since her rebirth as a nation. "Finally, fanatic Islam," wrote Clarence H. Wagner, Jr. in *Dispatch from Jerusalem*, "which has active programs for the takeover of nations from N. Africa to the Philippines, is certainly not going to back down on the crown jewel, Israel. A powerful Jewish state, in what they see as Islamic territory, will never be accepted by Islam, no matter how much money or benefits the western world tries to offer. Fanatic Islam's answer to western global power and influence was September 11, 2001" (July-Aug. 2002).

SUGGESTED ORDER FOR SMALL GROUPS

APPROACHING WITH PRAISE AND WORSHIP

Choruses of prayers of praise, thanksgiving and adoration

PRAYER TIME

Prayers of confession, petition & intercession

BIBLE WARM-UP: The Old Testament Names of God

Finding a Firm Foundation in a Rapidly Changing World

Jehovah-shalom (je-ho-vah-sha-lom): God our Peace.

MEMORY VERSE

1 Samuel 16:7 *"The LORD said to Samuel, 'Do not consider his appearance or his height, for I have rejected him. The LORD does not look at the things man looks at. Man looks at the outward appearance, but the Lord looks at the heart*

DAILY BIBLE READINGS: WORDS & THOUGHTS FOR FURTHER REFLECTION

Day 1: Isaiah 44:12-28

Day 2: Isaiah 45:1-14

Day 3: Isaiah 45:15-25

Day 4: Isaiah 46

What in Heaven's Name is Happening on Earth?

_____
    _____

Day 5: Isaiah 47

_____
    _____

Day 6: Isaiah 48

_____
    _____

Day 7: Isaiah 49:1-13

_____
    _____

DISCUSSION QUESTIONS

1. Do you agree that there is a propaganda war going on right now regarding Israel and the Palestinians?

Finding a Firm Foundation in a Rapidly Changing World

2. Read Jeremiah 33:23-26. What are the chances, according to these verses, of God reneging on His Covenant with Abraham and Israel? Discuss.

3. According to the two Palestinian officials mentioned in the text, what are the goals and strategies of the Arab nations?

4 . Discuss the U.S. sponsored "Road Map to Peace" as mentioned in the text. What nations are in the "Quartet" and how much of the world does it represent. See Zechariah 12:3.

5   Compare what Zechariah prophesied some 2,500 years ago in Zechariah 12:2-3, 6 and these words by Egyptian President Hosni Mubarak in March 2001 as reported by *Newsweek* magazine regarding negotiations between Israel and the Palestinians: "Let me tell you, the most dangerous issue is not this. It's Jerusalem. Jerusalem can stop everything….I don't think he [Arafat] will accept. Jerusalem is one reason…You cannot imagine what public opinion was like here. I had warnings, don't ever sign anything concerning Jerusalem and the holy places." Would you agree that Zechariah sounds as up to date as *Newsweek?*

6. Notice Luke 21:24. According to the text, what does the phrase "until the times of the Gentiles are fulfilled" mean and what significance has the date June 1967?

7.Why is Jerusalem "an immovable rock" to both Jews and Muslims in the negotiations regarding "land for peace"?

CLOSING PRAYER: Father, we pray for the peace of Jerusalem and for your people in Israel and throughout the world. We look for your appearing, Lord Jesus, and pray that you'll find us faithful and true and joyfully doing our Master's business. In these last of the last days, our Father, we pray for the greatest harvest of souls for Christ in all of history. Help us not to miss getting in on your harvest, Lord, but may we be able to lay at your feet all that we are and have and allow nothing or no one to hinder us. Break the chains that would bind us, O Lord! Free us up so that we can be desperate for your Presence and power! In the Precious and Powerful Name of the Lord Jesus, we pray. Amen.

Finding a Firm Foundation in a Rapidly Changing World

CHAPTER TEN

GOD WILL PROVIDE FOR OUR PROTECTION

But now, God's message, the God who made you in the first place, Jacob, the one who got you started, Israel: 'Don't be afraid, I've redeemed you. I've called your name. You're mine. When you're in over your head, I'll be there with you. When you're in rough waters, you will not go down. When you're between a rock and a hard place, it won't be a dead end – Because I am God, your personal God, The Holy of Israel, your Savior. I paid a huge price for you: all of Egypt, with rich Cush and Seba thrown in! That's how much you mean to me! That's how much I love you! I'd sell off the whole world to get you back, trade the creation for you. So don't be afraid: I'm with you.

Isaiah 43:1-5 (The Message)

For such a time as this, we need to know about God's protection and what He has provided for us. The Apostle Paul's exhortation to the Ephesian Christians is as timely for us as it was for them. He wrote, 'Finally be strong in the Lord and in his mighty power. 11 Put on the full armor of God so that you can take your stand against the devil's schemes. 12 For our struggle is not against flesh and blood, but against the rulers, against the authorities, against the powers of this dark world and against the spiritual forces of evil in the heavenly realms"(Ephesians 6:10-12).

Let's examine this passage a little closer. In this final exhortation to the Ephesian Christians, the apostle Paul zeroes in on the great spiritual struggle that every Christian finds himself or herself in once they have been born again. Paul never leaves any doubt about the believer's ongoing warfare against the enemy and for advancing the kingdom of light. He urged his son in the faith, Timothy, to "endure hardship with us like a good soldier of Jesus Christ" (2 Timothy 2:3) and to "fight the good fight of the faith. Take hold of the eternal life to which you were called when you made good your confession in the presence of many witnesses" (1 Timothy 6:12) And when close to death, with gratitude to God, he could say, "I have fought the good fight...I have kept the faith" (2 Timothy 4:7)

KNOW WHAT IT MEANS TO BE "IN" THE LORD

So, as he has been emphasizing all through Ephesians about being "in Christ" and "in the Lord", he concludes with one more: be strong in the Lord! (vs 10). First of all, let me suggest that to be "strong" in the Lord is to know what it means to be "in" the Lord.

To be "in" the Lord is to experience salvation by grace through faith (Ephesians 2.4-10). It is to know that this gift of salvation includes past, present and future: that we have been delivered from the penalty of sin(past), from the power of sin (present), and one day will be saved from the very presence of sin (future). Paul teaches that in the letter to the Romans (6:1-23; 8:18-25). It is also to experience salvation as the work of God the Holy Spirit from the new birth (John3:3) to the working out of our salvation every day (Philippians 2:12-13) to being equipped for the Lord's service (Acts 1:8).

Secondly, I think to be "strong in the Lord" is to know His "mighty power" (vs 10). Notice what it is NOT: it is not being extremely knowledgeable about God or the Bible. Theologians and Bible scholars often know much about God and the Bible but could not be described as "strong" in His power (James tells us that the demons believe in God in James 2:19). It is not being able to talk easily about the Lord Jesus or the Christian faith because many who glibly called "Lord, Lord" will not be given entrance to heaven (Matthew 7:21-22). It is not having a gift or gifts of the Holy Spirit because the gifts are given—they're gifts!—and are given without regard to spiritual depth.

KNOW WHAT IT IS TO BE STRONG IN HIS "MIGHTY POWER

What is His "mighty power"? It seems to me that it is the opposite of worldly strength, wisdom or values. "For the message of the cross is foolishness to those who are perishing," wrote Paul," but to us who are being saved it is the power of God...For the foolishness of God is wiser than man's wisdom, and the weakness of God is stronger than man's strength" (1 Corinthians 1:18, 25).[74]; see also Isaiah 55:8-9; 2 Cor. 12:9-10; 13:4)

[7474] See also Isaiah 55:8-9; 2 Corinthians 12:9-10;13:4.

The measure of His "mighty power or strength" in our lives, I believe, is seen in the degree to which we are led and governed by God the Holy Spirit. I think that's what is meant by being strengthened "with power through His Spirit in your inner being" in Ephesians 3:16 and having the love of God "poured into our hearts by the Holy Spirit" in Romans 5:5. It is also measured by the degree to which we consistently exhibit the fruit of the Holy Spirit in our lives (Galatians 5:22-23). And, of course, our Lord's "mighty power" is seen in the miracles, signs and wonders that have always accompanied the spreading of the Gospel throughout the world.

In speaking about God's "mighty power" Paul knew whereof he spoke, because it accompanied his apostolic ministry: "Therefore I glory in Christ Jesus in my service to God. I will not venture to speak of anything except what Christ has accomplished through me in leading the Gentiles to obey God by what I have said and done—by the power of signs and miracles, through the power of the Spirit. So from Jerusalem all the way around to Illyricum, I have fully proclaimed the gospel of Christ. It has always been my ambition to preach the gospel where Christ was not known, so that I would not be building on someone else's foundation" (Romans 15:17-20).

KNOW THE NATURE OF THE ENEMY

With Roman soldiers all around him, guarding him and being chained to him at times, Paul was familiar with the armour worn by Roman soldiers. He envisions each disciple of Jesus having spiritually that kind of armour available to him for protection when assaulting the enemy. Note that the armour is for taking a "stand against the devil's schemes" (vs 11). It is for active combat against the enemy!

I've heard numbers of soccer coaches urge the team to get to know as much as possible about their opposite number on the opposing team – it's smart to know your enemy! That's what Paul is doing here in this passage. He's revealing the nature of the struggle and the enemy. We'd be wise to know the nature of our enemy, the devil.

To begin with, learn his various designations. Here's a good sample:

- the ruler of this world: Ephesians 6:11

- the prince of the power of the air: Ephesians 2:2

- the god of this age: 2 Corinthians 4:4

- angel of light: 2 Corinthians 11:14

- a roaring lion: 1 Peter 5:8

- the adversary: 1 Timothy 5:14

- the slanderer and liar: John 8:44

- the accuser of the brethren: Revelation 12:10

The enemy is never human beings – "it is not against flesh and blood". It is the "devil's schemes" and the devil himself that we must take a stand against. Paul gives us an example of what that could be in a practical sense in 2 Corinthians 2:9-11 "The reason I wrote you was to see if you would stand the test and be obedient in everything. If you forgive anyone, I also forgive him. And what I have forgiven…I have forgiven in the sight of

Christ for your sake, in order that Satan might not outwit us. For we are not unaware of his schemes." Paul's teaching here is that to leave a matter unresolved and unforgiven is to give the enemy a foothold to work his devious schemes in our lives.

All the best Bible translations agree that Ephesians 6:12 is referring to different classes of evil spirits and demons: "For our struggle is not against flesh and blood…" The struggle is "against the rulers, against the authorities, against the powers of this dark world and against the spiritual forces of evil in the heavenly realms"; "persons without bodies – the evil rulers of the unseen world; those mighty satanic beings and great evil princes of darkness who rule this world, huge numbers of wicked spirits in the spirit world" (Living Bible); "organizations and powers that are spiritual…the unseen power that controls this dark world, and spiritual agents from the very headquarters of evil" (J.B. Phillips); and "cosmic powers, the authorities and potentates of this dark world, the superhuman forces of evil in the heavens" (New English Bible).

Satan is not omniscient (all knowing) nor is he omnipresent (present everywhere) as God is; the devil needs all the help he can get! So the evil spirits and the demons are his subordinates and extensions of himself. In verse 12 we have Satan's organization of his underlings in a hierarchy of authority and power. Michael Green, Anglican Bishop and recognized scholar, has an insightful comment on this: "In Matthew 25:41, Jesus speaks of 'the devil and his angels,' clearly indicating demonic powers. In Revelation 16:13-14 it is plain that demons and unclean spirits are identical; they are lieutenants of Satan. The Beelzebub controversy puts the matter beyond doubt (Matt. 12:22-29). The Pharisees charged Jesus with casting out demons through Beelzebub, the prince of demons, and Jesus rebutted their charge. But both parties agreed on the nature of these unclean spirits: they derive from the Unholy spirit himself" [75].

He goes on to say that "words like principalities, powers, thrones are used both of human rulers and of the spiritual forces which lie behind them. This is readily demonstrable. Luke 12:11 clearly refers to men when it says 'when they bring you before the synagogues and the rulers and authorities. [also Acts 4:26]. On the other hand, it is perfectly manifest that the powers and thrones and authorities in Colossians 1:16; 2:15; Romans 8:38, Ephesians 6:12 are superhuman powers"[76]

"And that about wraps it up," to quote *The Message* rendering of Ephesians 6:10-12, "God is strong, and he wants you strong. So take everything the Master has set out for you, well-made weapons of the best materials. And put them to use so you will be able to stand up to everything the Devil throws your way. This is no afternoon athletic contest that we'll walk away from and forget about in a couple of hours. This is for keeps, a life-or-death fight to the finish against the Devil and all his angels."

PUT ON THE FULL ARMOR OF GOD

---

[75] M.Green, *I Believe in Satan's Downfall* (Grand Rapids, Michigan: Eerdmans Publishing Company,1981), pp. 83-84.

[76] *Ibid*.

Paul goes on to list the different parts of the armor provided for each believer in Ephesians 6:13-18

"Therefore put on the full armor of God, so that when the day of evil comes, you may be able to stand your ground, and after you have done everything to stand. 14 Stand firm then, with the belt of truth buckled around your waist, with the breastplate of righteousness in place,15 and with your feet fitted with the readiness that comes from the gospel of peace. 16 In addition to all this, take up the shield of faith, with which you can extinguish all the flaming arrows of the evil one. 17 Take the helmet of salvation and the sword of the Spirit, which is the word of God. 18 And pray in the Spirit on all occasions with all kinds of prayers and requests."

Whether we like it or not, once we commit our lives to the Lord Jesus and are new creations in Christ, we are at war with the enemy of our souls, Satan or the devil or the evil one. *"Therefore, take up God's armour; then you will be able to stand your ground when things are at their worst, to complete every task and still to stand"* (vs. 13 NEB). Because we have an enemy and we are at war with him, we need protective armour and defensive and offensive weaponry.

However, protection and weaponry are of little value to us unless we have a strategy in place. Let me suggest a strategy to go along with the armour and weaponry of God: (1) Proclaim Christ's victory on the Cross as often as possible and especially when under pressure (1 Corinthians 1:18; Colossians 2:12-15); (2) Close your life to evil but see to it, make sure that you open it to God the Holy Spirit, that is, schedule time throughout the week for worship, praise, prayer and reading and studying the Bible, and fellowshipping with others who love the Lord Jesus (Romans 6:11-13); finally, (3) utilize your resources!

a. Seek Spiritual gifts and ministries and be really serious and committed about it. Why? Among other important reasons, because you'll find your growth will accelerate in the all-important "fruit of the Spirit" when you seriously seek and exercise spiritual gifts and ministries (Galatians 5:22-6:5).

b. Learn the triumphal shout: YOU, LORD JESUS ARE THE LORD ALMIGHTY AND YOU REIGN! And do it especially when the battle seems to be going against you! (Joshua 6:16, 20; 1 Samuel 4:5-6; Ezra 3:11-13).

c. Accentuate the positive, emphasize what unites (Ephesians 4:1-3); and, lastly,

d. Put on the armour of God with prayer:

-put on the belt of truth (vs 14): this was the belt from which hung the soldier's sword and which gave freedom of movement. What wonderful freedom there is in knowing that Jesus is "the truth"! (John 14:6)

-put on the breastplate of righteousness: accusations come to naught when we live righteously! (vs 14)

-put on the sandals (or boots!), which speak of eagerness and readiness to share the gospel of Jesus with others (vs 15).

-take up the shield of faith: "The word which Paul uses is not the word for the comparatively small round shield. It is the word for the great oblong shield which the heavily armed warrior wore. One of the most dangerous weapons in ancient warfare was the fiery dart. It was a dart tipped with tow dipped in pitch. The pitch-soaked tow was set alight, and the dart was thrown. But the great oblong shield was the very weapon to quench it. The shield was presented to the dart, the dart sank into the wood, and naturally the flame was put out." Strong faith can handle easily "the flaming arrows of the evil one" (vs 16).

-take the helmet of salvation: the enemy fears the human mind and intellect and makes it his business to bring into captivity as many as possible of the institutions and methods of informing, developing and educating the human mind. The gift of salvation is like a helmet protecting us from his lies (vs. 17).[77]

-take the sword of the Spirit, "the word of God": This is the only offensive weapon mentioned and it is the only one needed – remember how the Lord Jesus thwarted the devil's attack in Luke 4 "it is written….it is written….it says". Hebrews 4:12 has this confirming word: "For the word of God is living and active. Sharper than any double-edged sword…it judges the thoughts and attitudes of the heart."

PRAY! PRAY! PRAY!

Paul's closing exhortation is all about prayer. He challenges them and us to "pray" in the Spirit on all occasions with all kinds of prayers and requests" (vs 18). 1 Corinthians 14:2, 12-18 encourages us to pray in the Spirit as the Holy Spirit directs my spirit (see also Jude 20)

---

[77] See also 2 Corinthians 10:3,5.

Finding a Firm Foundation in a Rapidly Changing World

He urges them and us "to keep on praying for all the saints" and to "be alert" (vs18) The Bible challenges us to keep alert and to beware of a number of things:

(1) Keep alert and don't forget the Lord – "beware lest you forget the Lord" who redeemed you (Deut. 6:12; 8:11);

(2) Keep alert by remembering that prophets, preachers and people are not always what they claim to be – "beware of false prophets, who come to you in sheep's clothing...You shall know them by their fruits" (Matt. 7:15-16; 10:16-17; also 2 Peter 3:14-18);

(3) Keep alert by being aware of the dangers of formalism and naturalism – "beware of the leaven of the Pharisees..." (Matt. 16:6-12; Mark 8:15; Luke 12:1-3) and "beware of the scribes..." (Luke 20:46-47: Mark 12:38-40; also 2 Timothy 3:1-5);

(4) Keep alert by being on guard against the subtleties of materialism – "Take heed and beware of covetousness: for a person's life consists not in the abundance of things possessed" (Luke 12:15, 16-21); and,

(5) Keep alert by always realizing the unlimited nature and the limitless capacity of the power and love of God (1 John 3:1; 4:10).

Paul concludes the letter by asking for prayer for himself:

"And don't forget to pray for me. Pray that I'll know what to say and have the courage to say it at the right time, telling the mystery to one and all, the Message that I, jailbird preacher that I am, am responsible for getting out. Tychicus, my good friend here, will tell you what I'm doing and how things are going with me. He is certainly a dependable servant of the Master! I've sent him not only to tell you about us but to cheer you on in your faith. Goodbye, friends. Love mixed with faith be yours from God the Father and from the Master, Jesus Christ. Pure grace and nothing but grace be with all who love our Master, Jesus Christ." (*The Message*, vs. 19-24).

SUGGESTED ORDER FOR SMALL GROUPS

APPROACHING WITH PRAISE AND WORSHIP

Choruses of prayers of praise, thanksgiving and adoration

PRAYER TIME

Prayers of confession, petition & intercession

BIBLE WARM-UP: The Old Testament Names of God

Jehovah-tsidkenu (je-ho-vah tsid-kay-noo): God our Righteousness

MEMORY VERSE

Revelation 1. 5b-6 "To him who loves us and has freed us from our sins by his blood, and has made us to be a kingdom and priests to serve his God and Father – to him be glory and power for ever and ever! Amen."

DAILY BIBLE READINGS: WORDS & THOUGHTS FOR FURTHER REFLECTION

Finding a Firm Foundation in a Rapidly Changing World

Day 1: Isaiah 49:14-26

_____
_____

Day 2: Isaiah 50

_____
_____

Day 3: Isaiah 51:1-11

_____
_____

Day 4: Isaiah 51:12-23

_____
_____

Day 5: Isaiah 52

_____
_____

Day 6: Isaiah 53

Day 7: Isaiah 54

_____
_____

DISCUSSION QUESTIONS

1. Read Ephesians 6:10-12. Describe what you think a Christian who is "strong in the Lord" would look like.

2. Paul tells us clearly that the enemy is not "flesh and blood", not other human beings. Discuss how our relationships might be improved if we could always remember that.

3. Compare 2 Corinthians 11:13-15 and 1 Peter 5:8. What situations or events or happenings would you classify as the devil in "angel of light" roles and which might be his "roaring lion" roles? Can you think of any biblical examples?

4. Read Ephesians 6:13-18. Why did Paul urge us to put on "the full armour of God"? (see vs. 11, 13)

5. Discuss the suggested strategy of closing our lives to worldly things but opening them to the Lord and to the gifts of the Holy Spirit. (See Romans 6:11-14)

6. The shield of faith is a fascinating piece of the armour of God. Discuss how our faith can shield us from the "flaming arrows of the evil one". Give some examples of what the "flaming arrows" might be.

7. What part of the body does the armour not protect? Why?

CLOSING PRAYER: Heavenly Father, we acknowledge your great and mighty power and give you praise that you reign over all. We praise you that no evil can come near us or befall us that you have not defeated and from which you will deliver us . Thank you for the protection of your armour and the gift of your Holy Word. Lord Jesus, thank you for purchasing for us such a full and free Salvation by your Death and Resurrection. You are worthy of all our praise and adoration! Thank you, Holy Spirit, for coming into our lives and enabling us to love and serve the Lord Jesus. In the Strong Name of Jesus, we pray. Amen.

What in Heaven's Name is Happening on Earth?

CHAPTER ELEVEN

CHRIST WILL COME AGAIN FOR US!

The return of Christ will signal not only the Father rescuing his children but also the Bridegroom rescuing the Bride. As the church, we're part of the ultimate Cinderella story – rescued from a home where we labor, often without appreciation or reward. One day we'll be taken into the arms of the Prince and whisked away to live in his palace.

Randy Alcorn[78]

If there is an air of unreality, clouds of doubt and skepticism about Jesus coming to this earth the first time, I'm sure you'll agree that when it comes to His Second Coming the air is thick with scorn and the clouds are black with unbelief. I must admit that Christ's Second Coming at times does seem too

---

[78] *HEAVEN* (Carol Stream, Illinois:Tyndale House Publishers, 2004), p. 199.

good to be true: a fantasy birthed out of our wishful thinking and imagination. When it comes to our Lord's Return, there are lots of sceptics out there asking if it is really true. But the Bible replies loud and clear: "Yes, there really is a Second Coming!" The interest in it is so widespread that *Time* magazine ran its July 1, 2002, issue with a white Cross emblazoned on the cover with the words "THE BIBLE & THE APOCALYPSE" on the Cross. The sub-heading was "Why more people are reading and talking about THE END OF THE WORLD." The following article covered 13 pages out of a total of 54. The article zeroed in on the fact that Tim LaHaye's and Jerry Jenkins' *Left Behind* Series most recent publication had sold 3 million copies that year!

JESUS WILL COME AGAIN!

The Bible clearly and persistently states that the Lord Jesus will come again. This time, however, the Lord of the Universe will not come as He came the first time, incognito as a carpenter's baby, but as the Lord of Lords and King of Kings. He will not come as a child to grow and develop but as the legitimate rightful and powerful heir of His Father's world and universe. This is how He will come the second time:

- not to heal and to forgive but to judge, to make right what is wrong, and to straighten what is crooked.
- not to suffer, but to rule and reign over all.
- not to start and to establish a Church but to finish, to bring to an end the work of the Church He died for.
- not to call and commission His followers but to commend and to crown those who faithfully served Him.
- not to return to Nazareth, a city lowest of the low, but to Jerusalem, to Zion, the City of God.

- not to be at the mercy of religious and political authorities, or at the whim of puppet kings and Roman Emperors but to rehabilitate all kinds of power under His Lordship so that from this time on power will never be experienced without love and justice; power will emanate and flow from the One who is pure and perfect love. Earth will receive her King and His Peace and Love will fill the universe.

Notice these three general statements about our Lord's Return: One, it is a dominant theme in the New Testament and is described in detail in Matthew 24, Mark 13, Luke 21, John 14, Acts 1, 1 Thessalonians 4-5, 2 Thessalonians 2 and Revelation 19-20, to name those that come to mind. Two, it is a foundational Christian doctrine and Christians of every stripe preach and teach it. Three, it is to be looked for with joyful anticipation. In Matthew 24 the disciples asked the Lord Jesus what the signs of His coming again would be and for the next 20 verses He revealed them. He then says in verses 32-33: "Now learn this lesson from the fig tree: As soon as its twigs get tender and its leaves come out, you know that summer is near. Even so, when you see all these things, you know that it is near, right at the door." Again, in Luke 21:27 "When these things begin to take place, stand up and lift up your heads, because your redemption is drawing near." In other words, when you see these signs "begin" to take place, stand up and lift up your head in joyful anticipation of my Coming Again!

SIGNS OF HIS COMING AGAIN

What were these signs that would indicate that His Coming was "right at the door"? Matthew 24:4-31 gives a detailed list: verse 4, watch out for deceivers claiming to be the Christ; verse 6, be aware of wars and rumours of wars but don't worry, the end is still to come; verses 7-8, watch for the beginning of birth pains like nations rising against nations, kingdoms against kingdoms along with famines and earthquakes; verses 9-12, other signs will be persecution, heresy and apostasy; verse 14, when the whole world has heard the Gospel, the end will be just around the corner; verses 15-22, keep watch for 'the abomination that causes desolation' standing in the holy place, as foretold by Daniel; verses 23-28, be vigilant for false Christs and false prophets performing great signs and miracles. We must remember that we are to stand up and lift up our heads when these things BEGIN to take place!

The apostle Paul taught more about the Second Coming than any other writer in the New Testament. He especially addresses the subject in 1 and 2 Thessalonians. The Christians in the city of Thessalonica had some questions about the Second Coming and erroneously thought that the Lord would definitely return before any of them died. When that did not happen, because some of them did die, a controversy arose among them about the destiny of those who died before the Lord Jesus returned.

It seems to me that Paul has three words for these believers. He has A WORD OF COMFORT in 1 Thessalonians 4:13-18, A WORD OF WARNING in chapter 5:1-9 and A WORD OF CLARITY in 2 Thessalonians 2:1-2.

A WORD OF COMFORT

He begins to address the subject in 1 Thessalonians 4:13-18 "Brothers, we do not want you to be ignorant about those who fall asleep, or to grieve like the rest of men, who have no hope. 14 We believe that Jesus died and rose again and so we believe that God will bring with Jesus those who have fallen asleep in him. 15 According to the Lord's own word, we tell you that we who are still alive, who are left till the coming of the Lord, will certainly not precede those who have fallen asleep. 16 For the Lord himself will come down from heaven, with a loud command, with the voice of the archangel and with the trumpet call of God, and the dead in Christ will rise first. 17 After that, we who are still alive and are left will be caught up together with them in the air. And so we will be with the Lord forever. 18 Therefore encourage each other with these words." Let's look a little closer at this passage.

Paul immediately puts to rest the thought that these believers who had died, had died just like any other people. In verse 13 he states clearly that Christians need not "grieve like the rest of men, who have no hope" because Christ is our hope and life. Therefore, Paul declares that those believers who die before His Second Coming will come with the Lord when He returns to earth.[79]

In verses 15-17 he outlines the order of our meeting the Lord when He comes: (1) those who have died will come with Him and will experience the resurrection of the body; (2) those believers who have not died will be "caught up" (or "raptured") to meet the Lord "in the air". Commentators mention that the phrase "in the air" often refers to the abode of evil spirits and demonic powers and that its use here is

---

[79] See John 14:1-6; 2 Corinthians 5:1-10.

underscoring the Lord's supreme victory over the powers of darkness. It will be the place of this awesome UNION with the Lord Jesus and our amazing re-union with all those loved ones who have gone before. The implication is that the Lord will meet His people "in the clouds" and will proceed on with His blood-washed throng to claim the earth as His own. For Paul there is nothing more to add: "And so we will be with the Lord forever"(vs.17) We will be with the Lord forever! No wonder Paul concludes with "encourage each other with these words."

A WORD OF WARNING

Paul now turns from answering the question about those believers who die before the Lord's Return to another concern of the Thessalonians: When will the Lord Jesus come back to earth?

He addresses this in chapter 5:1-9 "Now, brothers, about times and dates we do not need to write to you, 2 for you know very well that the day of the Lord will come like a thief in the night. 3 While people are saying, 'Peace and safety,' destruction will come on them suddenly, as labor pains on a pregnant woman, and they will not escape. 4 But you, brothers, are not in darkness so that this day should surprise you like a thief. 5 You are all sons of the light and sons of the day. We do not belong to the night or to the darkness. 6 So then, let us not be like others, who are asleep, but let us be alert and self-controlled. 7 For those who sleep, sleep at night, and those who get drunk, get drunk at night. 8 But since we belong to the day, let us be self-controlled, putting on faith and love as a breastplate, and the hope of salvation as a helmet. (9) For God did not appoint us to suffer wrath but to receive salvation through our Lord Jesus Christ."

He begins by reminding them that he has no need to discuss "times and dates" with them, implying that he had covered that ground with them before, because they knew already that the Lord's Return would be like a "thief in the night." He goes on to discuss the impact of the Second Coming on those who don't believe in the Lord Jesus and on those who do.

To the world at large of unbelievers, His Coming will be totally unexpected–just as no one expects their home to be burglarized or their pocket to be picked. Furthermore, it will be for them sudden destruction (vs.3): "sudden" because it will happen when they are arrogantly boasting of "peace and safety", scornful of all that is Christian and Godly, entrenched in their religion, secularism and materialism. The picture in Matthew 24 and Luke 21 is of something like the roof of the world falling in and everything becoming unglued. The Lord Jesus warned His disciples about upheavals in the earth and sky at His Coming Again. And not just destruction of property – but "painful" destruction as intense as the labour pains of pregnancy (1 Thess. 5:3) and just as certain and without escape. What a terrible and horrendous time for a Christ-rejecting world! The constant message of the Bible, therefore, is understandable – flee to Jesus! Make no delay! Tomorrow may be too late! Accept and embrace Him now! The consequences of dying without Him or of not having embraced Him before His Coming are too horrible to take chances. No betting man in his right mind would take the odds: eternity is an awful long time to spend absolutely alone, separated from God and all that is peaceful, loving and good. Thus the urgency of the Bible: "NOW is the time of God's favour. NOW is the day of salvation" (2 Corinthians 6:1-2).[80]

Paul then reminds the Thessalonians that, in contrast to unbelievers, there is no excuse for Christians to be caught napping at the Lord's Return (5:4-8). They have been told of His Coming and the need for vigilance lest they be acutely embarrassed by not being ready for His Return (vs.4). The repetition of this call to vigilance regarding Christ's Coming to Christians in Rome and Ephesus underscores its importance and that our apathy and lethargy about it is a major weakness that the enemy constantly probes and exploits.[81] Paul continues his appeal to them using further contrasts: they are of the darkness, you are of the light; they are the children of the night, you are the children of the day; they are asleep, you must be awake (vs. 5-7). And stay awake: "Let us be alert and self-controlled," exhorted Paul in verse 6.

In 5:8-11 he urges the Thessalonians to add to vigilance virtue and put on "faith and love as a breastplate, and the hope of salvation as a helmet" (vs. 8). The language Paul is using here, of course, is that of warfare. We are engaged in spiritual warfare at every turn and Paul never ceases to remind us of that (see Romans 13:12; 2 Corinthians 6:7, 10:4; Ephesians 6:13ff for other refs. to armour). There are no more important pieces of armour than the breastplate and the helmet – one covers and protects the heart, the other the mind. The more faith and love we live out, the better our hearts are protected from the enemy's darts and thrusts; the more often our

---

[80] See also Isaiah 13:6-13.

[81] See Romans 13:11-14; Ephesians 5:6-21.

thoughts dwell and muse on the wonderful hope or expectation of salvation, the less likely we are to succumb to the lies and deceit of Satan. And what is the hope of salvation? It is nothing other than the glorious appearing of our Lord and Saviour Jesus Christ!

Verse 9 is a key verse in discussing the whole topic of future things or eschatology. We must never forget while we're speaking of God's judgment and wrath on the earth – like the Flood, Sodom and Gomorrah – that God has not appointed us "to suffer wrath but to receive salvation through our Lord Jesus Christ." When the world's cup of iniquity has overflowed, when the last Gentile or Jew has completed the Bride of Christ, and God says "Enough is enough!" then He will withdraw His people and save them from His wrath – as He did with Noah and Lot and their families. The Scriptures, it seems to me, offer no more information than that regarding when the Lord Jesus will remove the Church from the earth.

A WORD OF CLARITY

The rumour had spread and had been believed by some in Thessalonica that the Lord Jesus had already returned. Paul refutes this and gives some wise counsel about testing teachings that come our way. This is how he put it in 2 Thessalonians 2:1-12 "Concerning the coming of our Lord Jesus Christ and our being gathered to him, we ask you, brothers, (2) not to become easily unsettled or alarmed by some prophecy, report or letter supposed to have come from us, saying that the day of the Lord has already come. (3) Don't let anyone deceive you in any way, for that day will not come until the rebellion occurs and the man of lawlessness is revealed, the man doomed to destruction. (4) He will oppose and will exalt himself over everything that is called God or is worshipped, so that he sets himself up in God's temple, proclaiming himself to be God. Don't you remember that when I was with you I used to tell you these things? (6) And now you know what is holding him back, so that he may be revealed at the proper time. (7) For the secret power of lawlessness is already at work; but the one who now holds it back will continue to do so till he is taken out of the way. (8) And then the lawless one will be revealed, whom the Lord Jesus will overthrow with the breath of his mouth and destroy by the splendor of his coming. (9) The coming of the lawless one will be in accordance with the work of Satan displayed in all kinds of counterfeit miracles, signs and wonders, (10) and in every sort of evil that deceives those who are perishing. They perish because they refused to love the truth and so be saved. (11) For this reason God sends them a powerful delusion so that they will believe the lie (12) and so that all will be condemned who have not believed the truth but have delighted in wickedness."

Paul instructs these believers in verses 1-2 to stop their emotional, hysterical waiting for the Second Coming of Jesus and their "being gathered to Him." He tells them to judge every "prophecy, report or letter supposed to come from us" and to know that if it claims that the day of the Lord has come, it is false and a forgery.

It is important to notice the term "the day of the Lord". This is used throughout the Old Testament and there is no reason to believe that its meaning changes in the New Testament. The Lord Jesus was a Jew and also His apostles and likewise the first Christians – all of them accepted that "the day of the Lord" meant the end of time and the terrible judgment of

God upon the earth and when everything that was wrong would be made right.[82] The Jews believed that this would be the day of their ultimate salvation and, it seems to me, that all Paul does here is to include the Church or Christians whether Jew or Gentile. Indeed he equates "the coming of our Lord Jesus Christ and our being gathered to him" in verse 1 with "the day of the Lord" in verse 2.

He follows this with a warning every bit as relevant today as then: "Don't let anyone deceive you in any way". The Second Coming of the Lord has been a favourite doctrine of hucksters and tricksters for millennia! Not to mention its fascination for sincere extremists, fanatics and half-crazed prophets that history records with depressing frequency! Paul is saying here: "Listen and take note: there are some things that must happen before the day of the Lord occurs!"

Let's list and consider the things Paul mentions in verses 3-12:

1. "the rebellion"
2. "the man of lawlessness [or sin]"
3. "the one who holds back" the "man of lawlessness" (vs 6) and "lawlessness" (vs 7).
4. "the work of Satan"
5. "those who are perishing"

1. *"the rebellion"* (vs3): Ever since Adam and Eve, there has been rebellion in the world against the Lord. But Paul seems to be indicating a period of time in which rebellion against God will reach proportions and an extent never experienced before in

---

[82] See, for example, Isaiah 2:1-22; Ezekiel 39:7-11, 25-29; Joel 1:13-15; 2:1-11;28-32 (compare with Acts 2:14-21).

human history. I would suggest that we are in such a time as never before have human beings had thecapacity in wealth and technology to commit sin on increasingly grander scales (e.g., nuclear and biological weaponry; pornographic filth in books, movies, videos, TV programming; exploitation of the poor by the wealthy in adult and child prostitution tourism, etc.).

2. *"the man of lawlessness,"* also called "the man of sin" (vs 3-4): This is clearly a reference to an individual who would later be called "the antichrist" by the Apostle John (1 John 2:18-23, 4:3; 2 John 7; see also Revelation 13:1-18). The thought seems to be that as the Lord Jesus was the "incarnation" of God at the beginning of the last days, so the antichrist will be the "incarnation" of Satan or evil at the end of the last days. Paul tells the Thessalonians that this man will be "revealed" and is "doomed to destruction". He will oppose God and exalt himself, even taking over God's temple and proclaiming himself to be God. He will be worshipped and embraced by those who reject the Lord Jesus (vs. 10).

The Antichrist will be a charming, powerful religious and/or political figure who has effective, plausible answers for worldwide political, economic and social problems. Probably a Middle East leader who will gain the confidence of Israel and the Arab states, but in the end will betray Israel and her allies, eventually bringing all the armies of the Arab world and their allies against Jerusalem.

3. *"the one who holds back...."* (vs 6-7): There is much difference of opinion about whom Paul is referring to here. The Thessalonians had no problem understanding it as Paul had taught them about this in person, according to vs. 5. Some think he is referring to the Roman Emperor, as the head of State and the pinnacle of authority. Others that he is speaking of the ,Holy Spirit. If he is referring to the authority of the State, then it does fit with the reign of lawlessness or the "secret power of

lawlessness" of vs. 7. So that another sign to look out for as a harbinger of the Lord's Return would be the diminishing power of the State and widespread lawlessness. (It is interesting to notice Genesis 6:11-13 that God judges the earth because of widespread "violence").

4. *"the work of Satan"* (vs9): The antichrist will rise to prominence on a sea of "counterfeit miracles, signs and wonders," the outward expression of the work of Satan. There is no doubt about it: we are hearing and seeing claims of more miracles, signs and wonders than ever before in human history – not surprisingly in one sense because of the worldwide communication systems we now enjoy. How do we discern what is the work of God and what is the work of Satan? We must be awake and watchful. We must ask questions such as:

-Do I know the person making the claim is a person of integrity?

-Is the Lord Jesus the ONLY ONE being exalted in this claim?

-Does its context have the marks of the world about it, i.e. Hollywood hucksterism? etc. etc.

(See also Matthew 7:21-23; Revelation 19:11-16, 19-20).

5. *"those who are perishing"* (v10): Those whom the enemy deceives by hindering them from believing and embracing the Lord Jesus as Saviour, by blinding them to truth and salvation and enabling them to believe a "powerful delusion (vs 11). What could the "powerful delusion...the lie" be? It has to be a worldwide delusion since Paul is speaking of

antichrist, "the man of lawlessness" (vs. 3). Could it be that the materialist, secularist West, that has rejected its evangelical Christian heritage, will embrace Islam that already encircles the world and claims almost one and a half billion followers? Could it be that the talk about restoring the Islamic Caliphate or Empire by a charismatic leader who will unite the two competing, mutually hostile sects of Islam, the Sunnis and Shias, will be more than talk?

The President of Iran, Mahmoud Ahmadinejad, right at this time, believes and proclaims that he has been chosen to prepare the way for the Twelfth Imam, the Islamic Messiah. "He told associates," states Rosenberg, "that he believed the end of the world was just two or three years away. He said he believed he had been chosen by Allah to become Iran's leader at this critical hour to hasten the coming of the Islamic messiah known as the Twelfth Imam or the Mahdi by launching a final holy war against Christians and Jews." Not in the least shy about letting the world know about his special calling, Ahmadinejad closed his speech to the United Nations General Assembly on September 17, 2005 with a prayer: "O mighty Lord, I pray to you to hasten the emergence of your last repository, the Promised One, that perfect and pure human being, the One that will fill this world with justice and peace."[83]

Paul's closing words to his first letter to the Thessalonians provide us with an appropriate conclusion: "May God himself, the God who makes everything holy and whole, make you holy and whole, put you together – spirit, soul and body – and keep you fit for the coming of our Master, Jesus Christ. The One who called you is completely dependable. If he said it, he'll do it!" (5.23-24 The Message)

---

[83] J. C. Rosenberg, *EPICENTER: Why the Current Rumblings in the Middle East will Change your Future* (Carol Stream, Illinois: Tyndale House Publishers, 2006), pp. X-XI.

Finding a Firm Foundation in a Rapidly Changing World

SUGGESTED ORDER FOR SMALL GROUPS

APPROACHING WITH PRAISE AND WORSHIP

Choruses or prayers of praise, thanksgiving & adoration

PRAYER TIME

Prayers of confession, petition & intercession

BIBLE WARM-UP: The Old Testament Names of God

Jehovah-rohi (je-ho-vah ro-ee): God our Shepherd

MEMORY VERSE

Zechariah 12:10 *"And I will pour out on the house of David and the inhabitants of Jerusalem a spirit of grace and supplication. They will look on me, the one they have pierced, and they will mourn for him as one mourns for an only child, and grieve bitterly for him as one grieves for a firstborn son."*

DAILY BIBLE READINGS: WORDS & THOUGHTS FOR FURTHER REFLECTION

Day 1: Isaiah 55

What in Heaven's Name is Happening on Earth?

_____
_____

Day 2: Isaiah 56

_____
_____

Day 3: Isaiah 57

_____
_____

Day 4: Isaiah 58

_____
_____

Day 5: Isaiah 59

_____
_____

Day 6: Isaiah 60

_____
_____

Finding a Firm Foundation in a Rapidly Changing World

Day 7: Isaiah 61

_____

_____

DISCUSSION QUESTIONS

1. Read 1 Thessalonians 4:13-18. What should our attitude be towards death? How should we think of it? How do you think a funeral for a believer should differ from a funeral for an unbeliever? Share any other thoughts you may have about this passage.

2. Read 1 Thessalonians 5:1-9. What do you think Paul means by saying that the Second Coming ought not to be a surprise to believers? Discuss.

3. Do you think the average Christian would be surprised by the Lord's Return? What could we do to remove this element of surprise in the Second Coming?

4. Read 2 Thessalonians 2:1-12. Do you think Paul's caution to the Thessalonian believers about accepting too quickly statements or ideas about the Return of the Lord Jesus is appropriate for our time as well? Discuss.

5. What was the erroneous teaching about Christ's Return that had come to the Thessalonian Church? Any suggestions as to why it might arise at this time?

6. How does Paul describe the Antichrist? Putting his description in your own words, what would he look like on our modern international stage?

7. What does the Second Coming of the Lord Jesus mean to you personally? Do you think about it with some apprehension and fear? Or with expectation or joy? With mixed feelings? Discuss. See John 14:1-6.

CLOSING PRAYER: Come, Lord Jesus, King of Kings and Lord of Lords, reign in our hearts, reign in our homes, reign in our Church, reign in our City, reign in our nation, reign in our world. Come, Lord Jesus, great and mighty God and wonderful loving Saviour, come and reign over us that we might be fully free of this clinging sinful nature and be freed to love you and all you've created with a pure love, without spot or stain. As we look for the signs of your Coming, Lord, please give us eyes to see and open receptive hearts. In the Name that is above all names, Jesus, we pray. Amen.

What in Heaven's Name is Happening on Earth?

CHAPTER TWELVE
A NEW HEAVEN AND A NEW EARTH

When referring to this place, Christians often talk about living with God 'in heaven' forever. But in fact the biblical teaching is richer than that: it tells us that there will be new heavens and a new earth – an entirely renewed creation – and we will live with God there.

Wayne Grudem[84]

One of the most read – and heard at almost every funeral service – is John 14. 1-6: "'Do not let your hearts be troubled. Trust in God; trust also in me. In my Father's house are many rooms; if it were not so I would have told you. I am going there to prepare a place for you. And if I go and prepare a place for you, I will come back and take you to be with me that you also may be where I am. You know the way to the place

---

[84] Grudem, p. 1158.

What in Heaven's Name is Happening on Earth?

where I am going. Thomas said to him, 'Lord, we don't know where you are going, so how can we know the way?' Jesus answered, 'I am the way and the truth and the life. No one comes to the Father except through me.'" These words have brought immeasurable comfort to bereaved families down through the centuries. They have also strengthened and encouraged millions upon millions of persecuted and oppressed followers of Jesus with their message of the return of their Lord: "I will come back and take you to be with me that you also may be where I am. You know the way to the place where I am going." The message they heard was "Don't be discouraged, hold on! I'll be there for you to take you to my place! Don't lose hope!"

The Second Coming of the Lord Jesus for most Christians is as far as their eschatology reaches. After that we go to Heaven. Period. Unfortunately information about what we see and what happens next for many Christians comes from old jokes about Saint Peter and the pearly gates. We cringe when somebody cracks the one about the wise guy who asks a gathering of Christians if they believe in Heaven; then to put up their hand if they want to go there. When all the hands go up, he then pulls out a handgun and tells them to step up and he will answer their prayers. Of course, the punch line of the joke is that nobody steps up – the assumption being that no one really believes in heaven or we wouldn't wait to get there.

The surprising and amazing thing is that the Bible has so much to say about Heaven – about its inhabitants and what they do and say there, and about its nature, significance and importance. It is clear that to the Bible writers it was real, physical, and tangible. But, someone will say, Heaven is completely spiritual. And that is true: Heaven is spiritual, but in the same sense that the Resurrected body of our Lord was clearly physical and spiritual. He walked and talked and ate with the disciples and was accepted by them as obviously human, and yet he entered the room "though the doors were locked" and seemed to be able to appear and disappear at will (Luke 24.13-31; John 20.26) "Talk of 'heaven' and 'earth', though," observes Bishop N.T. Wright, renowned author and scholar, "comes to us from the Bible; and in the Bible these are not two places, separated from each other by many miles, but two different *dimensions* of the total reality of the world....so 'heaven' and 'earth' are the two dimensions of created reality. These two God-given dimensions interlock and interact in a variety of ways, sometimes confusingly, often surprisingly. And it's particularly important to notice that heaven and earth were both created good." [85]

Wright, in another book, emphasizes the importance of understanding that heaven and earth overlap and ultimately both will become one. "The New Testament picks up from the Old the theme that God intends, in the end, to put the whole creation to rights. Earth and heaven were made to overlap with one another, not fitfully, mysteriously, and partially as they do at the moment, but completely, gloriously, utterly. 'The earth shall be filled with the glory of God as the waters cover the sea.' That is the promise which resonates throughout the Bible story, from Isaiah (and behind him, by implication, from Genesis itself) all the way through to Paul's greatest visionary moments and the final chapters of the book of Revelation." He goes on to

---

[85] N.T. Wright, *The Millennium Myth* (Louisville, Kentucky: Westminster John Knox Press, 1999), pp.36-37.

What in Heaven's Name is Happening on Earth?

quote a stanza from the beloved old hymn "This is my Father's World," reminding us that this is not a new teaching:

This is my Father's world; O let me not forget

That though the wrong seems oft so strong,

God is the ruler yet.

This is my Father's world; the battle is not done;

Jesus, who died, shall be satisfied,

And earth and heaven be one[86].

So where is heaven? In another dimension that may be closer to us than we can imagine.

I wonder if we find it so hard to believe that heaven will come to earth, and all that is good and beautiful on earth will remain and be all the more good and beautiful , because we think it is too good to be true - because we've bought into pagan Greek philosophy that only the spirit is good and that matter is evil. We end up thinking that only the spirit realm is good and that the material, physical world is bad. Randy Alcorn, pastor, theologian and best-selling author, in his comprehensive study of *Heaven,* calls this *Christoplatonism* and defines it as follows: "Plato, the Greek philosopher, believed that material things, including the human body and the earth, are evil, while immaterial things such as the soul and Heaven are good. This view is called Platonism. The Christian church, highly influenced by Platonism through the teachings of Philo

---

[86] N.T. Wright, *SIMPLY CHRISTIAN: Why Christianity Makes Sense* (New York, NY: HarperCollins Publishers, 2006), pp.217-218.

Finding a Firm Foundation in a Rapidly Changing World

(ca. 20 BC-AD 50) and Origen (AD 185-254), among others, came to embrace the 'spiritual' view that human spirits are better off without bodies and that Heaven is a disembodied state. They rejected the notion of Heaven as a physical realm and spiritualized or entirely neglected the biblical teaching of resurrected people inhabiting a resurrected Earth." He goes on to say that "Christoplatonism has had a devastating effect on our ability to understand what Scripture says about Heaven, particularly about the eternal Heaven, the New Earth".[87]

But the truth is the curse imposed on the old Creation because Adam and Eve rebelled will have been removed and we'll be living in a pre-Fall Eden-like environment. In all likelihood it will be superior to Eden because of the all-encompassing, comprehensive Victory of our Lord Jesus over the evil one and his kingdom. If Eden was a literal paradise, why should we not believe that the New Earth will be just as literal?

What will help us in our understanding of the Scriptural teaching on Heaven is recognizing what the theologians call the "present or intermediate" Heaven. In using that term, they are referring to the place believers go at death: Absent from the body is to be "at home with the Lord" (2 Cor. 5:8). It is the Heaven we reside in until the Second Coming of our Lord to Earth and the New Heaven and New Earth. One significantly important difference, of course, between the intermediate Heaven and the New Heaven is that we'll have our resurrected bodies, which we receive only at the Second Coming. Further differences are that the New Heaven and New Earth are eternal, and that the curse of the Fall will be removed completely and forever.

---

[87] R. Alcorn, *HEAVEN* (USA: Tyndale House Publishers, Inc, 2004), p. 52.

What in Heaven's Name is Happening on Earth?

It is of tremendous help in grasping the biblical doctrine of Heaven to know which Scriptures refer to the intermediate or present Heaven and which to the eternal or New Heaven. The most important thing we know of the intermediate Heaven is that we'll be with the Lord. Though it will be far superior to anything we've yet experienced, it is still not our final destination. It is not the final place the Lord has been preparing us for and will prepare for us. That will be the New Heaven and New Earth. "Though it will be a wonderful place, the present Heaven is not the place we are made for – the place God promised to refashion for us to live in forever," writes Alcorn, "God's children are destined for life as resurrected beings on a resurrected Earth. We must not lose sight of our true destination. If we do, we'll be confused and disoriented in our thinking about where, and in what form, we will spend eternity."[88]

What will the eternal Heaven be like? Will the old earth be destroyed? Will we be capable of sinning? Will Heaven ever be boring? No, Alcorn answers to those questions, referencing many Bible texts , while answering affirmatively to many others that all of us have: Will the New Earth be familiar – like home? Will we actually rule with Christ? Will there be space and time? Will the New Earth have sun, moon, oceans, and weather? Will we be ourselves? Will we eat and drink on the New Earth? Will there be marriages, families, and friendships? Will animals inhabit the New Earth? Will animals, including our pets, live again? Will there be arts, entertainment, and sports? Will our dreams be fulfilled and

---

[88] Alcorn, p. 42.

Finding a Firm Foundation in a Rapidly Changing World

missed opportunities regained? Alcorn answers a resounding Yes to all of those.

If we die before the Lord Jesus returns, we will go immediately into the Presence of our Lord – the intermediate Heaven. We will return with Him or, if still living on earth, caught up to meet Him, and will receive our resurrected bodies. As resurrected servants of Christ, we will reign with Him as He governs the Earth as King of Kings and Lord of Lords for the millennium period (obviously the curse still has not been removed on Earth as sin and death are evident). The millennium ends with the release of Satan and his final rebellion against God, ending in his annihilation. The Day of Judgment follows and then the New Jerusalem descends from Heaven. Since it seems the New Jerusalem was created before the New Heaven and New Earth, some have suggested that the New Jerusalem might have hovered above the Earth as a huge satellite city inhabited by those who were resurrected and who travelled back and forth as they reigned with Christ on Earth. This would help explain where the millions and millions of resurrected believers are during the millennium.[89] Nevertheless, with the coming of the New Jerusalem eternal Heaven begins and God's amazing Plan of Salvation is accomplished.

What in Heaven's Name *will be happening* on Earth? God will prepare a place for us to dwell with Him forever, the New Heaven and New Earth. Heaven will be brought to a New Earth and God's glory will fill the Universe. "The physical heavens are constantly declaring God's glory (Psalm 19:1-2). Even now, in reference to an Earth under the Curse," observes

---

[89] J.F. Walvoord, *Every Prophecy of the Bible* (Colorado Springs, Colorado: Chariot Victor Publishing, 1999), p. 632

Alcorn, "God says, 'The glory of the Lord fills the whole earth' (Numbers 14:21). But the universe will behold an even greater display of God's glory, one that will involve redeemed men and women and redeemed nations on a redeemed earth. It is on Earth, God promises, that 'the glory of the Lord will be revealed, and all mankind together will see it' (Isaiah 40:5)"[90]

THE NEW HEAVEN AND THE NEW EARTH

We began this study by referring to Genesis 1-2 and the story of Creation and the commissioning of Adam and Eve, the first two chapters of the Bible. Significantly, the last two chapters of the Bible climax the whole story of God's plan and purpose for His children and His Universe with an account of this new Creation. Let's look more closely at these two chapters as we conclude our study of God's work of Salvation and loving intervention in our World.

REVELATION 21:1-4

1 Then I saw a new heaven and a new earth, for the first heaven and the first earth had passed away, and there was no longer any sea. 2 I saw the Holy City, the new Jerusalem, coming down out of heaven from God, prepared as a bride beautifully dressed for her husband. 3 And I heard a loud voice from the throne saying, "Now the dwelling of God is with men, and he will live with them. They will be his people, and God himself will be with them and be their God. 4 He will wipe every tear from their eyes.

---

[90] Alcorn, pp.93-94.

There will be no more death or mourning or crying or pain, for the old order of things has passed away."

What a relief for John to turn from the terrible, horrible visions of Satan's destruction and the great white throne Judgment in the previous chapter to see a new heaven and a new earth, an earth without any seas. The idea of a new heaven and earth would not have been new to John as it is mentioned at least twice in the Old Testament, even though in the context of the millennium. "Behold, I will create new heavens and a new earth," declared the Lord in Isaiah 65:17-18, "the former things will not be remembered, nor will they come to mind. But be glad and rejoice forever in what I will create, for I will create Jerusalem to be a delight and its people a joy." The next five verses describe the millennium including the wolf and the lamb feeding together. Walvoord points out that in prophecy events that are distant in time from one another often are spoken of in the same context. He mentions as examples those scriptures that join together the first and second comings of the Lord Jesus in Isaiah 61:1-2 (cf. Luke 4:17-19) and Malachi 4:5-6[91] . What is clear is that we are now in the realm of eternity.

In verse two we learn that the new earth includes the New Jerusalem "coming down from God out of heaven, , prepared as a bride beautifully dressed for her husband." Notice the contrast between the earthly Jerusalem being called Sodom spiritually in 11:8 and this New Jerusalem "the Holy City". Again, the thought of the New Jerusalem would have been familiar to John as it had been a dream of the Jews for centuries. Other dreams and visions had come to previous

---

[91] Walvoord, pp. 311-312.

priests and prophets and included the streets and buildings of gold, precious stones, gates of splendor, no need of the natural light of the sun and moon because God Himself will be the light, and the coming of nations to Jerusalem bearing gifts.[92]

Strange as the symbolism is in describing the city as a beautifully attired bride, it was not unfamiliar as it is used in Isaiah 52:1-2 "Put on your garments of splendor, O Jerusalem, the holy city." Just as the great whore could symbolize Babylon/Rome as all who opposed and rejected the Lord, so the beautiful Bride symbolized by the New Jerusalem represents all the people down through the ages, Jew and Gentile, who loved and obeyed and were faithful to the Lord. This seems to be the meaning of the names of the tribes on the twelve gates and the names of the apostles on the twelve foundations of the City in verses 12-13. Of course to say that is not to deny the literal and physical New Jerusalem existing on earth. There is no reason why it can't also represent all the redeemed who ever lived. After all a throne represents kingship and kingdom but is also used as a seat for the monarch.

Verse 3 announces that God will now dwell among His people. This time not incognito as the son of a carpenter but openly: "He will live with them. They will be his people, and God himself will be with them and be their God." And because the Lord God is the One who paid the price of their redemption, it is He who "will wipe every tear from their eyes" and will remove from them "death and mourning or crying or pain, for the old order of things has passed away" (vs. 4).

---

[92] Barclay, p. 258.

Finding a Firm Foundation in a Rapidly Changing World

REVELATION 21:9-21

9 One of the seven angels who had the seven bowls full of the seven last plagues came and said to me, "Come, I will show you the bride, the wife of the Lamb." 10 And he carried me away in the Spirit to a mountain great and high, and showed me the Holy City, Jerusalem, coming down out of heaven from God. 11 It shone with the glory of God, and its brilliance was like that of a very precious jewel, like a jasper, clear as crystal. 12 It had a great, high wall with twelve gates, and with twelve angels at the gates. On the gates were written the names of the twelve tribes of Israel. 13 There were three gates on the east, three on the north, three on the south and three on the west. 14 The wall of the city had twelve foundations, and on them were the names of the twelve apostles of the Lamb. 15 The angel who talked with me had a measuring rod of gold to measure the city, its gates and its walls. 16 The city was laid out like a square, as long as it was wide. He measured the city with the rod and found it to be 12,000 stadia in length, and as wide and high as it is long. 17 He measured its wall and it was 144 cubits thick, by man's measurement, which the angel was using. 18 The wall was made of jasper, and the city of pure gold, as pure as glass. 19 The foundations of the city walls were decorated with every kind of precious stone.... 21 The twelve gates were twelve pearls, each gate made of a single pearl. The great street of the city was of pure gold, like transparent glass.

In a strange and striking twist the angel, who probably was the one in 17:1 who invited John to see the punishment of the great prostitute, now comes and invites him to see "the bride, the wife of the Lamb". So John is whisked away in the Spirit and shown the Holy City, the New Jerusalem, coming down from heaven and shining with the brilliance of the glory of God "like that of a very precious jewel, like a jasper, clear as crystal" (vs. 10-11). John describes this heavenly scene in the best of earthly terms and uses the rarest of jewels and precious stones, the jasper – a bright quartz, a lustrous green – to convey the dazzling radiance and splendour of God's holy presence.

Verses 12-14 focus on the number 12 and convey an important message the Church has needed to hear from its very beginning. There were 12 gates, three facing each direction of the compass, and on the gates the names of the 12 tribes of Israel. The wall of the city had 12 foundations bearing the names of the 12 apostles of the Lamb. Both Israel and the Church are represented here. The Church did not replace Israel as God's people but together they are the people of God. The names of the tribes and the apostles on the same wall of the Holy City speak eloquently to this truth – that the promises of God to Israel are integrated with the Gospel of the Lord Jesus Christ in birthing one Community of God's People.

The immensity of the City is mind-boggling (vs. 15-17). It is a perfect cube measuring 1,500 miles in each direction including its height. That's an astonishing 2,250,000 square miles, calculates one commentator, and that it would very nearly stretch from London to New York across the Atlantic ocean. He deduces from this that the uppermost message being conveyed is that there will be room for everyone. No one need feel excluded or left out: the choice is completely theirs.[93]

In verses 18-21 there are various references to gold and precious stones. The City shines and glitters like "pure gold, as pure as glass". The walls are studded with every kind of precious stone; the gates are made of pearl; and the city's main street is "of pure gold, like transparent glass". But the main

---

[93] Barclay, p. 271.

point of all this seems to be that it is a backdrop to the glorious Presence and Light of God Himself.

REVELATION 21:22-27

22 I did not see a temple in the city, because the Lord God Almighty and the Lamb are its temple. 23 The city does not need the sun or the moon to shine on it, for the glory of God gives it light, and the Lamb is its lamp. 24 The nations will walk by its light, and the kings of the earth will bring their splendour into it. 25 On no day will its gates ever be shut, for there will be no night there. 26 The glory and honor of the nations will be brought into it. 27 Nothing impure will ever enter it, nor will anyone who does what is shameful or deceitful, but only those whose names are written in the Lamb's book of life.

This City had no temple and no need of one because "the Lord God Almighty and the Lamb are its temple." What a radical change for Jews and Christians! Our worship has always focused on a building of some description, even though we've known that God's Presence cannot be contained in an earthly dwelling. In the New Jerusalem God and the Lamb will be its temple. Perhaps that is what is most significant about the perfect cube shape of the Holy City: in the Jewish faith the cube spoke of heavenly and holy things. In Solomon's temple, the Holy of Holies was a perfect cube and the cube shape occurs over and over again in Ezekiel's visions of the new Jerusalem and the new temple.[94]

Furthermore, the City has no need of manufactured or natural light because God's glory is the light and the Lamb is the lamp. Therefore, there is no need of sun or moon. These

---

[94] 1 Kings 6:20; Ezekiel 41:21; 43:16; 45:2; 48:20. Barclay, 271.

are some of the details when "the dwelling of God is with men, and he will live with them. They will be his people, and God himself will be with them and be their God" (21:3). All the nations and their kings will be drawn to its light and will "bring their splendor" and their "glory and honour...into it".

There will be no need to shut the City gates because there will be no evil or enemies or fear of the dark. The glorious Presence of God and the Lamb will never leave, so there will be no night there! Nor will anything or anyone impure enter it "but only those whose names are written in the Lamb's book of life". One commentary points out that "Because the whole city has replaced the Temple, the city is like a temple to the rest of the earth. The people of the city are the priestly people to the whole earth. But who else is on the earth but not in the city? The answer is not clear.... What is clear is that nothing evil, nothing unclean, will be able to contaminate or corrupt the new Jerusalem." [95]

REVELATION 22:1-5

1 Then the angel showed me the river of the water of life, as clear as crystal, flowing from the throne of God and of the Lamb 2 down the middle of the great street of the city. On each side of the river stood the tree of life, bearing twelve crops of fruit, yielding its fruit every month. And the leaves of the tree are for the healing of the nations. 3 No longer will there be any curse. The throne of God and of the Lamb will be in the city, and his servants will serve him. 4 They will see his face, and his name will be on their foreheads. 5 There will be no more night. They

---

[95] C.G. Gonzalez & J.L Gonzalez, *REVELATION* (Louisville, Kentucky: Westminster John Knox Press, 1997), pp. 142-143.

will not need the light of a lamp or the light of the sun, for the Lord God will give them light. And they will reign for ever and ever....14Blessed are those who wash their robes, that they may have the right to the tree of life and may go through the gates into the city.

To this point the exterior dimensions and description of the Holy City have been the subject at hand. Now our attention is directed to the interior. Down the main street of the City will flow the river of the water of life, clear as crystal, and flowing from the throne of God and of the Lamb. On each side of this river, the tree of life will produce a crop of fruit every month and its leaves "are for the healing of the nations". We read of a similar picture in Ezekiel 47:1, 12 of the river that flows from the temple and in Zechariah 14:8 of the living water that will flow east and west, in summer and winter, during the millennium. But this river of life flows in eternity and probably symbolizes eternal life and life in the Holy Spirit as promised by the Lord Jesus in John 7:38, 39; 10:10 and fully experienced in the new Jerusalem. It symbolized eternal life just as the Temple in the Old Testament symbolized the Presence of God. The whole scene in the verses 1-2 are reminiscent of Genesis 2:9-10, reminding us that the water and tree of life are now in the context of a city or in a city garden or park.

There will be no evil in the Holy City. The central focus will be the throne of God and of the Lamb. His servants will see His face and will bear His name and serve Him forever, even as the beast's servants bore his mark and perished. Notice God and the Lamb are worshipped together in the light of their Presence.

What in Heaven's Name is Happening on Earth?

    Over and over again, the book of Revelation specifies certain blessings or beatitudes. The seventh and last one is "blessed are those who wash their robes, that they might have the right to the tree of life and may go through the gates into the city" (other beatitudes are in 1:3, 14:13, 16:15, 19:9, 20:6, 22:7). This blessing is referring to God's free gift of salvation through the blood of our Lord Jesus that gives the right to the tree of life and to go through the gates of the city. I'm reminded of the old Gospel hymn:

What can wash away my sin?

Nothing but the blood of Jesus!

What can make me whole again?

Nothing but the blood of Jesus!

O Precious is the flow

That makes me white as snow,

No other fount I know

Nothing but the blood of Jesus!

    What in Heaven's Name is happening on Earth? God is fulfilling His Plan for the universe, for all of His Creation that fell under sin's curse. Adam and Eve's rebellion did not catch Him by surprise: He had a Plan of Salvation already in place. Not for a moment did Satan ever have the upper hand: right from the beginning , when our first parents used their free will to ruin their complete lordship over the Earth, God never abandoned His Plan for them to rule the earth. His Plan was nothing less than the complete restoration of His whole Creation. All that has been and is and will be happening on our Earth, in *Heaven's Name,* has as its objective the New Heaven and the New Earth. At the centre and heart of that Plan is the all-conquering God the Son, our Lord Jesus Christ, King of Kings and Lord of Lords.

This Scriptural summary of God's Plan of Salvation provides us with an appropriate conclusion: "Praise be to the God and Father of our Lord Jesus Christ! In his great mercy he has given us new birth into a living hope through the resurrection of Jesus Christ from the dead, and into an inheritance that can never perish, spoil or fade – kept in heaven for you, who through faith are shielded by God's power until the coming of the salvation that is ready to be revealed in the last time. In this you greatly rejoice, though now for a little while you may have had to suffer grief in all kinds of trials. These have come so that your faith – of greater worth than gold, which perishes even though refined by fire – may be proved genuine and may result in praise, glory and honor when Jesus Christ is revealed. Though you have not seen him, you love him; and even though you do not see him now, you believe in him and are filled with an inexpressible and glorious joy, for you are receiving the goal of your faith, the salvation of your souls. Concerning this salvation....you know that it was not with perishable things such as silver or gold that you were redeemed...but with the precious blood of Christ, a lamb without blemish or defect. **HE WAS CHOSEN BEFORE THE CREATION OF THE WORLD, BUT WAS REVEALED IN THESE LAST TIMES FOR YOUR SAKE"** (1 Peter 1:3-20. Emphasis added.)

What in Heaven's Name is Happening on Earth?

SUGGESTED ORDER FOR SMALL GROUPS

APPROACHING WITH PRAISE AND WORSHIP

Choruses or prayers of praise, thanksgiving & adoration

PRAYER TIME

Prayers of confession, petition & intercession

BIBLE WARM-UP: The Old Testament Names of God

Jehovah-shammah (je-ho-vah sham-mah); God the Ever-Present One, the God who is there.

MEMORY VERSE

Zechariah 14:8a-9 *"On that day living water will flow out from Jerusalem... The LORD will be king over the whole earth. On that day there will be one LORD, and his name the only name."*

DAILY BIBLE READINGS: WORDS & THOUGHTS FOR FURTHER REFLECTION

Finding a Firm Foundation in a Rapidly Changing World

Day 1: Isaiah 62

_____
_____

Day 2: Isaiah 63

_____
_____

Day 3: Isaiah 64

_____
_____

Day 4: Isaiah 65:1-12

_____
_____

Day 5: Isaiah 65:13-25

_____
_____

Day 6: Isaiah 66:1-11

_____
_____

What in Heaven's Name is Happening on Earth?

Day 7: Isaiah 66:12-24

_____

_____

DISCUSSION QUESTIONS

1. What did John see and hear in Revelation 21:1-4?

2. From these verses, describe what heaven will be like?

3. The Lord said to John in Revelation 21:6 "it is done" or "it is finished": What did He mean and where in the Bible have we heard those words before?

4. What are the rewards mentioned here for knowing and loving the Lord and what are the consequences for rejecting Him and following Satan? (21: 6-8)

5. The Holy City, New Jerusalem, represents the Bride of Christ. What significance is there in the elaborate and extravagant description of the City (jewelry, precious stones, mind-boggling dimensions of 1,500 miles x 1,500 miles x 1,500 miles)? (21:9-21)

6. What is the significance of the names of the 12 tribes of Israel and the 12 apostles being on the gates and the wall?

7. Why does the Holy City not need natural light or a temple in it? (21:22-27)

CLOSING PRAYER: Heavenly Father, thank you for this time we've had together studying your Word. Thank you for what you've taught us and for your loving and gracious promises to us. Help us to live our lives in the expectation of your Coming Again, Lord Jesus. Holy Spirit, please keep reminding us that time is short and that every day is a loving gift from our Father. Amen. Come, Lord Jesus!

Finding a Firm Foundation in a Rapidly Changing World

What in Heaven's Name is Happening on Earth? Is an attempt to understand the current turmoil in our twenty-first century world. Though by no means exhaustive, it examines the broad themes of redemption and salvation, themes that run throughout the Bible. Its premise is that there is more going on than meets the eye and only from a Biblical perspective is there any hope of discerning and gaining insight into what is transitory and what is permanent, and what is temporal and what is eternal.

The Biblical message is that nothing is ever out of God's control and that even human hubris, greed and overweening ambition at their worst will never stop the inevitable fulfillment of His purposes and will. All of us are observers and participants in the dramas of life and THE DRAMA of life, God's plan of Redemption and Restoration – the drama that drives all the others – as it inexorably moves towards the eschaton, the end of an imperfect and fallen universe and the re-creation of a perfect and eternal one.

The Lord's Prayer is being and will be fulfilled literally: His *will* will be done on Earth as it is in Heaven; His *name* will be universally proclaimed and accepted as holy; His *kingdom* will be utterly victorious throughout the Earth and the universe; and evil in all its forms, including the evil one, will be destroyed and annihilated. There will be no more pain and suffering, no more disease and affliction, no more oppression and exploitation, no more war, no more sadness and tears. *With righteousness he will judge the needy, with justice he will give decisions for the poor of the earth….The wolf will live with the lamb, the leopard will lie down with the goat, the calf and the lion and the yearling together; and a little child will lead them. The cow will feed with the bear....They will neither harm nor destroy...for the earth will be full of the knowledge of the Lord as the waters cover the sea* (Isaiah 11:4-9).

ABOUT THE AUTHOR

WILLIAM (BILL) CALDERWOOD, PH.D., born and raised in N. Ireland, came to Canada as a young man. A pastor of many years' experience, he was the first pastor of River of Life Community Church in Lethbridge, Alberta, Canada, and currently serves as Pastor Emeritus. Dr. Calderwood is a Bible school graduate of Eston College, Saskatchewan, and holds degrees from the University of Saskatchewan in history and theology (B.A., M.A., B.D.) and from the University of London, England, in history (Ph.D.). He and his wife, Maidra, reside in Lethbridge, Alberta, Canada, and have three married children and seven grandchildren. During their many years of ministry in Lethbridge, they have also served the Lord in numerous overseas projects and missions.

Made in the USA
Charleston, SC
08 December 2012